USING BIBLICAL PATTERNS
TO UNLOCK END TIME EVENTS

USING
BIBLICAL PATTERNS
TO
UNLOCK
END TIME EVENTS

Mark S. Hoffmeister

Using Biblical Patterns To Unlock End Time Events

ISBN: 9781099740220

© 2019 Mark Hoffmeister

All rights reserved.

No part of this book may be used or reproduced, stored in a retrieval system, or transmitted in any form or by any means—electronic, mechanical, photocopy, recording, or any other manner—without the prior written permission from the author, except in case of brief quotations embodied in critical articles and reviews.

Unless otherwise noted, all Scripture passages are from the
King James Version of the Bible.

Holy Bible, New International Version, NIV, Copyright 1973, 1978, 1984, 2011 by Biblica Inc. Used by permission. All rights reserved worldwide.

DEDICATION

This book is dedicated to Jesus Christ,
the author of the biblical patterns, and to all those that look
to Jesus as their Rock in times of trouble.

ACKNOWLEDGEMENTS

I am grateful for Rob Lowenberg and his help in editing this book. Rob's persistent insights have helped me in the shaping of this manuscript and Rob's constant encouragement has helped me tremendously.

I also appreciate Heather Wilbur whose creative genius graces the cover.

I would like to thank my wife Kelly for her constant support during the time it took to write this book. Kelly has been a constant source of blessing and inspiration to me.

As always, I am thankful for the support of my children who have constantly encouraged me to continue writing.

TABLE OF CONTENTS

Dedication .... *v*
Acknowledgements .... *vii*

Chapter One 1
A Better Way to Gain Insight into End Time Events

Chapter Two 7
The Biblical Pattern Method for Interpreting Scripture

Chapter Three 19
Prophecies that Intersect the Biblical Pattern

Chapter Four 27
Hidden Deep within the Roman Empire

Chapter Five 35
The Seventh Beastly Kingdom

Chapter Six 47
The Fate of the Seventh Beastly Kingdom

Chapter Seven 57
The Rise of the Eighth Beast Empire

Chapter Eight 67
The Prototype Pattern for Revealing the Eighth Beast Empire

Chapter Nine 81
The Barrier to the Rise of the Eighth Beast Empire

Chapter Ten 91
The Dilemma of Saudi Arabia

Chapter Eleven 105
The Coming Showdown in Islam

Chapter Twelve 115
  The Emergence of the New Ottoman Empire

Chapter Thirteen 123
  The Gog, Magog War

Chapter Fourteen 137
  The Tale of Two Antichrists

Chapter Fifteen 153
  The Devastating Legacy of Gog

Chapter Sixteen 159
  The False Time of Peace

Chapter Seventeen 167
  The Biblical Pattern and Storyline for the Antichrist

Chapter Eighteen 179
  The Tyranny of the Antichrist

Chapter Nineteen 193
  The End of the Antichrist

Chapter Twenty 199
  The Rapture Pattern

Chapter Twenty-One 217
  America in Biblical Patterns

Chapter Twenty-Two 237
  Chaos Events

Chapter Twenty-Three 247
  Biblical Patterns—Messages for Our Time

About the time of the end, a body of men will be raised up
who will turn their attention to the prophecies,
and insist upon their literal interpretation, in the midst of
much clamor and opposition.

—Sir Isaac Newton

CHAPTER ONE

A Better Way to Gain Insight into End Time Events

Currently when discussions of end time events take place, we are faced with a quandary. How do we interpret the maze of scriptures dealing with this issue; and how do we arrive at a valid interpretation of what we are reading? In fact, should we even be having discussions of last day events at all?

It seems that as a Christian community we are very divided on these questions. If we are even willing to discuss end time events, we have formed into divergent camps of interpretations, usually based on different proponents and their points of view. Various interpretations have arisen; each with their scholars espousing their views and each based on sound biblical research. Over time, these interpretations have evolved into the unofficial doctrine of the Christian faith, albeit with a slightly Americanized slant. If anyone happens to disagree with the viewpoint generated by these interpretations, then they can be ostracized and labeled as someone that does not have a proper biblical world view.

We have even gone so far as to discount those who do not adhere to the accepted teachings we have come to believe. Instead of listening to a different perspective, we have become so entrenched in our deeply held beliefs that we become proponents of a view that may not be entirely correct. In essence, many have become like the Pharisees and Sadducees of Jesus time, unable to hear the truth because it does not support the popular religious world view. The Pharisees and Sadducees living in the time of Jesus could not even see the Son of God standing before them because He did not conform to what they thought He should be like. Have we inadvertently become like them because we cling to current biblical interpretations that may not express what God was trying to tell us? Are we so entrenched in our support for different scholastic opinions that we are unable to see a deeper level of meaning that has been in the Bible waiting for us to discover?

This has led us to our current situation. We are struggling to come to a proper interpretation of different areas in the Bible regarding end time events. There are many differing opinions, each supported by thorough biblical research, but each has generated more questions than answers. In the areas of the Bible where clear and explicit answers are not given in the text, we are still searching for ways the Bible has given us to properly interpret the disputed revelations. This has caused a considerable amount of confusion and conjecture. Let's look at an example. The Bible describes a series of beast kingdoms that arose on the earth in the past and were opposed to God's purposes and His people. (Daniel 7:3-7) By the time Jesus was born, five beast kingdoms had already come and gone. Jesus was living in the time of the sixth beast kingdom. Biblical scholars have identified all six of the beast kingdoms described in the Bible based on the characteristics described in the passages of prophecy. (We will discuss these later.) However, the Book of Revelation describes a mysterious seventh and eighth beast kingdom and does not tell us the identity of these two mysterious powers that come on the world stage after the death of Jesus.

Well-meaning researchers have poured over the scriptures and arrived at various conclusions as to the identity of the seventh and eighth beast kingdoms. All of these academics have provided sound biblical evidence for why they have arrived at their various conclusions, but it seems they cannot agree on the identity of the final two beast kingdoms. Some have told us that these final two powers are Rome. Others have told us that the United States is at least one of these two final world powers. Still others insist that a union of European nations comprise at least one of the last two empires. Instead of the Bible providing the identities of these two critical beast kingdoms, things have devolved into different denominations of Christians disputing over these key and decisive identities based on academic credentials and popularity.

There has got to be a better way to recognize what the Bible is referring to in crucial questions such as this one. Perhaps there is an overlooked method that can unite us in identifying critical areas in end time discussions, one that will remove debate and academic credentials from the criteria and set a clear blueprint for what to look for in these deliberations.

What if I were to tell you that there exists just such a method for ascertaining crucial biblical themes, and if you employ it you can unlock fundamental information that will allow you to discover the meaning of enigmatic end time passages? This technique allows the Bible to interpret itself by employing a seldom regarded method to unlock end time passages and divulge the true meaning of the text. In essence, this method becomes a cipher needed to unlock the messages concealed in the biblical text. If we employ this method of interpretation, we will discover an underlying blueprint for unlocking biblical verses and discover their relevance for the times we are living in today. In fact, by applying this biblical interpretation method, we will discover that the meaning concealed in the pages of the Bible is more relevant today than we could ever imagine! Even more, by using this method of biblical interpretation, we will be able to draw conclusions on how end time events will unfold, not based on what any individual person has to say, but based on what God has carefully concealed in His Word.

What is most astonishing about this method is that it is what the Bible tells us to do to unlock our understanding of future events. The Bible tells us if we want to discern the future, then we need to look at what happened in the past. "Tell us, you idols, what is going to happen. Tell us what the former things were, so that we may consider them and know their final outcome. Or declare to us the things to come." (Isaiah 41:22 NIV) God has concealed the future in patterns of things that have happened in the past. Discovering those patterns will unlock our understanding of end time events unfolding all around us.

Let's explore the biblical patterns that reveal the future together. Now more than ever, the relevance of what God has meticulously concealed in the Bible needs to be heard, and is waiting to be revealed to those who are honestly seeking the truth. God indeed has many things to say to the modern nations and to those people adrift and disconnected from Him and searching for meaning in the chaos they see around them in the world today.

CHAPTER TWO

The Biblical Pattern Method for Interpreting Scripture

Anyone who has ever read *The Harbinger* by Jonathan Cahn had to be amazed by a startling notion. God has hidden different patterns in the Bible by which He reveals His secrets, and He can use those same patterns in our modern world today to reveal modern day secrets. For those of you unfamiliar with this book (which I highly recommend you read), Rabbi Cahn describes the process by which judgment came upon ancient Samaria. The judgment came in a series of different patterns that occurred prior to the destruction of ancient Samaria. What was shocking to the readers of *The Harbinger* was the fact that the same series of patterns happened in New York City and the United States during the events of 9/11. Jonathan Cahn described these patterns as a biblical blueprint, a type of things to come, and a paradigm of things that had happened in the past and was happening in the United States. The astonishing fact is that the exact same patterns that happened so long ago in biblical times are manifesting today in our time in the United States!

Jonathan Cahn's latest work, *The Paradigm*, was equally as astounding when it revealed that the pattern surrounding the recent Presidential Election between Donald Trump and Hillary Clinton had played out in a similar fashion on an ancient stage recorded in the Bible. The cast of characters, the events that happened, and the circumstances they were involved in so closely paralleled ancient times that it almost defies imagination. Again, this is a book that you simply need to read. An ancient blueprint for the events that happened was described, and this same pattern, called a paradigm by Rabbi Cahn, was repeated in 2016 during the Presidential Election. The events so closely paralleled each other that they can only be described as astonishing, shocking and profound. What was the thing that tied these two separate events, separated by thousands of years together? It was a biblical pattern that was concealed in the Bible. The pattern was there in the Bible but was unrecognized and probably would never have been known if not by the inspired research and work of Jonathan Cahn.

If you have not heard much about biblical patterns before, you are not alone. While patterns in the Bible have been noted before, they have mainly been accepted as a peculiarity, an inadvertent coincidence or a mild amusement to be glossed over. Historians have recognized patterns in history and have observed that patterns have a history of repeating themselves. An example of this in the United States is the curious similarities between the presidencies of Abraham Lincoln and John F. Kennedy. Here are a few of the peculiar parallels between them.

The Biblical Pattern Method for Interpreting Scripture

There is an odd connection of 100 years between the two presidents. Abraham Lincoln was elected to congress in 1846, and then later to president in 1860. John F. Kennedy was elected to congress in 1946 and was elected president in 1960. The last names of both presidents have seven letters. The name of the man who succeeded President Lincoln was Johnson, Andrew Johnson. The name of the man who succeeded President Kennedy was Johnson, Lyndon Johnson. Both successors have thirteen letters in their first and last names. Andrew Johnson was born in 1808. Lyndon Johnson was born 100 years later in 1908. President Lincoln was killed by John Wilkes Booth and he was born in 1839. President Kennedy's assassin was Lee Harvey Oswald and he was born in 1939. The full names of John Wilkes Booth and Lee Harvey Oswald consist of fifteen letters. Both assassinated presidents were killed by a bullet to the head and their wives were with them. Both assassins were killed before they were tried in a court of law.

And still the coincidences go on. Booth killed President Lincoln in a theatre and then ran to a warehouse. Oswald killed President Kennedy from a warehouse and then took refuge in a theatre. President Lincoln was killed in Ford Theatre, and the car that was carrying President Kennedy when he was assassinated was a Ford, a Lincoln. President Lincoln's secretary was named Kennedy, and President Kennedy's secretary was named Lincoln. Both secretaries had begged their presidents not to go to the event that killed them. And finally, both presidents were killed on a Friday, one in 1863 and the other in 1963.

Are these all a mere series of coincidences or is there something deeper going on? It's almost as if in some things we were meant to notice the patterns, and then take a deeper look at them. It's time to take a closer look at some of the patterns hidden in the Bible and see if we can glean some information from them. If we can discover the relevant patterns, then a whole new world of understanding will be unlocked for us and we can begin to discover what will be facing us in the near future. It won't be the doctrines of men guiding us, but the hidden gems found deep within the Bible.

Unlocking the Beast Empires

The proper identification of the beast empires described in the Bible is of critical importance. The concept of a beast empire was first described in Daniel, chapter seven, where different animals were used to describe various pagan empires. If we don't know the correct identity of the first six beast empires, then we will never know the correct identity of the final two empires, and consequently we will never reach the appropriate conclusions regarding them. This is why there is so much confusion today on the beast empires.

First of all, for the sake of clarity, we need to define what a beast empire is. According to the Bible, and from the perspective of the Lord, a beast empire is a dominant world governmental ruling system that has sought to destroy the nation of Israel. If Israel did not exist as a nation at the time in question, then the beast empire would try to destroy the Jewish people. The Jewish people were selected by the Lord to be His chosen people and any attempt by any empire to destroy them is in direct opposition to God's will, regardless of whether the Jewish people are in the Lord's favor or not. In essence, a beast empire is the embodiment of Satan on the earth in certain ways and its actions as such would seek to carry out Satan's agenda through its earthly administrators during times of persecution. Satan is ultimately in control of these entities and as a consequence their agenda will reflect an attitude of trying to destroy God's plan and people.

Let's take a look at the early beast empires and see how they tried to destroy the Lord's people. The first one was the Egyptian Empire. Israel came into Egypt as a large family and then became a great nation while in captivity in Egypt for four hundred years. When it came time for people of Israel to leave Egypt, the Pharaoh would not let them leave as God intended. This led to the rise of Moses as the leader of Israel. The plagues of Egypt resulted from the refusal of Pharaoh to let the Israelites go. After Egypt had experienced the devastating plagues, Pharaoh relented and the Israelites fled. As they were leaving, the Pharaoh of Egypt had a change of heart and brought his chariots and troops to destroy the fleeing Israelites. As the Red Sea parted, the Israelites escaped the grasp of Pharaoh and his troops. The chariots and troops of Egypt did not experience the same saving grace. They were annihilated as the waters of the Red Sea rushed back in upon them. The destruction of the Egyptian army led to a turning point for all of Egypt. No longer would they ever be able to achieve their former status as a world power. From this point forward, Egypt was regarded as a third world nation, a mere footnote in the annals of history. The destruction Egypt wanted to inflict on the Lord's chosen people was returned upon them. This pattern then became a template for the rest of the beast empires following them. By his satanically inspired actions, the Pharaoh and nation of Egypt became the first beast kingdom.

The second beast kingdom was the Assyrian empire. The Assyrians moved in and destroyed the last vestiges of the Egyptian empire after the drowning of the Egyptian army in the Red Sea. They soon became the dominant power on the world stage. How did the Assyrian empire become regarded as a beast kingdom in the eyes of the Lord? It was by the actions of their leaders. The Assyrian king Shalmaneser laid siege to the ten northern tribes of Israel (2 Kings 17:4-6). The siege lasted three years, and was finished by the Assyrian King Sargon II in 722 BC when the last vestiges of Samaria (the ten tribes) were defeated. A little over twenty years later, the Assyrians under a new leader named Sennacherib came to finish the job of the destruction of Israel. Sennacherib brought a tremendous army of 185,000 troops with him. He laid siege to the city of Jerusalem. The Assyrian empire had already caused the deaths of countless thousands of Israelites when they destroyed Samaria, which were the northern ten tribes of Israel. Would they have success again against the remaining two tribes in the city of Jerusalem known as the Jewish people?

An astounding thing happened that ultimately led to the downfall of the Assyrian empire. The king of Judah named Hezekiah realized the predicament of the Jewish people and turned to God for help. Hezekiah repented of his sins, and then implored all of the people of Jerusalem to repent and to turn back to God. The people listened to Hezekiah, humbled themselves, and turned away from the things that were alienating them from God. When the Jewish people did this, the massive army of 185,000 Assyrians surrounding Jerusalem soon became a footnote in history. The Lord used supernatural intervention to destroy the army of Sennacherib in one night. The massive army of 185,000 men was all destroyed in one night by an angel of the Lord, and in the morning they were all dead corpses. (Isaiah 37:7, 36) Soon after this, the Babylonians finished the destruction of the Assyrian empire.

There is a noteworthy pattern beginning to develop here. A pagan empire arises, matures into dominant world status, and then persecutes the people of Israel or the Jewish people. God intervenes to save His chosen people, and the persecuting empire is soon annihilated and replaced by a newly arising pagan empire. The newly arising empire finishes the destruction of the old beastly kingdom and soon takes its power and becomes the new focus of power on the earth. Could this pattern happen again and become a template to recognize as other beastly kingdoms arose? Let's take a look.

The third pagan empire to arise was the Babylonians. Under the leadership of Nebuchadnezzar the Babylonians invaded the land of Israel and laid siege to the capital city of Jerusalem. This time the Jewish people did not turn back to God and were defeated and carried off into the land of Babylon. (2 Kings 24:11-14; 25:1-7) Estimates project that hundreds of thousands of Jews were killed by famine and warfare during the siege of Jerusalem. Were the Babylonians destroyed immediately because of the death and destruction they inflicted on the Jewish people? No they were not. God had another plan in mind when He allowed destruction to come to His chosen people. Nebuchadnezzar was given a dream that outlined his empire and three more beastly kingdoms that would follow him and dominate the world stage. In addition, the Jewish people were told that they would remain in captivity to Babylon for failing to keep the Shemitah years. Every seventh year on the Jewish calendar was set aside as a Shemitah year by the Lord and it was during this year that no labor or harvesting was supposed to take place. The Jewish people had failed to keep this commandment of the Lord 70 times and were allowed to remain in captivity for the 70 years they had failed to keep the commandment of the Shemitah year. At the end of the 70 years of confinement in Babylon, a curious thing happened. Another Babylonian ruler came to power after Nebuchadnezzar and mocked the Lord by foolishly using sacred Jewish temple implements in a pagan ritual. These implements were sacred and were not to be used sacrilegiously in pagan celebrations. This act showed utter contempt and disrespect for the Lord. The Lord did not ignore the disrespect shown to Him and that night the infamous writing on the wall appeared during a Babylonian feast. The Babylonian empire fell that night. This was the night that the Babylonian empire was held accountable for the hundreds of thousands of Jews that had perished during the reign of their beastly kingdom. It is not advisable to mock God and hold Him in contempt and derision. The implement of destruction of the Babylonian Empire was waiting right outside the gates of the city. That night King Cyrus and the Medo-Persian army managed to sneak inside the city of Babylon and conquered it in one night.

Is the biblical pattern of the beast empires holding? Yes it is, but it can be altered by the Lord and modified somewhat. The overall pattern is repeating. Another beast empire arises, defeats the old empire, then the new empire persecutes the people of God, that empire is held accountable for their actions, God intervenes, which leads to the collapse of the old empire, and then consequentially the new up and coming beast empire totally defeats the previous beast empire. In the case of the Babylonian empire, judgment was delayed because of other patterns the Lord had established and orchestrated to fit His perfect design. This is important to note—the pattern is holding but the Lord can alter it to fit His will.

Which empire became the fourth beastly kingdom? It was the same one that conquered the Babylonian empire. The Medo-Persian Empire arose the same day they had conquered Babylon. As recorded in the Bible, Cyrus, the new leader, helped portions of the Jewish people return to Jerusalem to begin rebuilding the temple. (2 Chronicles 36:22, 23) This was a noble effort and something that was ordained of God, but did the Medo-Persian Empire continue on this path of supporting the Jewish people? No they did not. They fell into the same pattern that turned other empires into beastly kingdoms in the eyes of the Lord. After a number of years, a plan was put into place to exterminate all of the Jewish people living in the Medo-Persian Empire. This devilish plot was designed by a man named Haman. Haman was an evil Persian viceroy who wanted to see all of the Jewish people killed. Haman devised a plot to exterminate all of the Jewish people on a certain date. This plan was discovered by the Jewish Queen Esther, and at considerable peril to her own life, the queen exposed the plot and convinced the king to repeal Haman's decree and save her people. The Lord intervened yet again through Queen Esther this time and saved His people from destruction. The Medo-Persian Empire did not last much longer after this event. A new leader arose on the scene and destroyed the Medo-Persian Empire. His name was Alexander the Great and he was the leader of the Grecian Empire.

Four times now this same biblical pattern has held. Four times it seems as if the Lord is telling us to notice this pattern and discern the way He is bringing about the rise and fall of these beastly kingdoms. Will we notice and look for the same pattern to repeat itself again or will we foolishly ignore what the Lord wants us to discern and watch for? Is it possible that this same blueprint will keep repeating itself? Let's delve deeper into this biblical pattern.

The next beastly kingdom to arise was the Grecian Empire. Alexander the Great was determined to be the conqueror of the world and had accomplished much of his plan until he died at an early age during his conquests. Other Greek kings arose in his place until a particular king committed an act that led to the downfall of the entire Grecian empire. The infamous leader was the Greek king Antiochus IV Epiphanes. He carried out a satanically inspired plan to eliminate the Jewish people and desecrate their temple. In 168 BC, he ordered the slaughter of 40,000 Jewish people, including the young and old and women and children. He sold another 40,000 Jews into slavery and then erected a statue dedicated to Zeus in the Jewish temple and ordered all Jews to worship Zeus. (2 Maccabees 5:11-14) This led to the Maccabean revolt where Judah Maccabee defeated the forces of Antiochus and freed the city of Jerusalem. It was during the time of the renewed dedication of the Jewish temple that the tradition of Hanukkah began when the Menorah burned miraculously for eight days when only one days' worth of oil was added to it. Soon after the defeat of Antiochus IV Epiphanes, Rome crushed the last remaining forces of the Grecian Empire and began their domination of the world. This would make Rome the sixth beastly empire in the biblical pattern.

Five beastly kingdoms had come and gone and five times the biblical pattern has held. The sixth empire, Rome, chose the same path as the other beast empires before them. This was the empire that Jesus Christ and all of the apostles operated in during their ministries. This is also the empire that dominated the world when Christianity began. What is unique about the

Roman Empire is that now you have two different groups that are looked after and protected by the Lord in a beastly empire. The first is the Jewish people, the chosen people of the Lord, and the second is the Christians, the people that have chosen the Lord Jesus Christ as their Savior. Rome persecuted both of these groups when they subjugated the Jewish people and destroyed Jerusalem in 70 AD, and later when they sacrificed Christians for in the Roman games in the coliseum for two centuries. The Roman Empire chose to persecute both the Jews and the Christians and in the end they would suffer the same fate as the other beastly empires. There are several important points that need to be made about the Roman Empire, the sixth beastly empire as identified by the biblical pattern.

Before we do that it might be helpful to list the first six beastly empires. They are:

1. Egyptian Empire
2. Assyrian Empire
3. Babylonian Empire
4. Medo-Persian Empire
5. Grecian Empire
6. Roman Empire

Important Points about the Sixth Beastly Empire, the Roman Empire

There are some critical concepts that we need to discuss about the Roman Empire. With just a cursory examination, it would appear as if the sixth beastly empire does not fit the biblical pattern established with the preceding five beast empires. For example, the previous empires were all destroyed almost immediately after they persecuted or tried to destroy the people of God. (Israel or the Jews) The Roman Empire carried out the destruction of Jerusalem and the slaughter and subjection of the Jewish people in 70 AD and later killed uncountable numbers of Christians in the Coliseum in the next two centuries. Yet they did not meet their fate until hundreds of years later. This begs the question, why the change in the pattern? What is happening?

Here are three very important points about biblical patterns:

1. Other prophecies can intersect with the biblical pattern and need to be fulfilled within the pattern.
2. Biblical patterns will hold true but can be delayed or modified to fit God's perfect will.
3. Timing of the biblical pattern depends upon the fulfillment of other prophecies within the pattern.

Let's discuss each of these points. These points are so important that we need to thoroughly examine each one of them.

CHAPTER THREE

Prophecies that Intersect the Biblical Pattern

We will begin with the fact that other biblical prophecies can interconnect and become incorporated within the biblical pattern. Earlier it was pointed out that the Babylonian empire did not follow the biblical pattern the way the Egyptian and Assyrian Empires did. The Egyptian and Assyrian beastly empires were almost immediately destroyed when they persecuted Israel. If that is the case, then what happened to change the pattern? We are given the answer in Leviticus in a series of passages that seem obscure to those of us in modern culture. In fact, most of us in the present day would read these passages and not give them a second thought. The passages I am talking about were given to the people of Israel and were meant to be a blessing to them while they were living in the land that God had set aside for them. Here is what the Lord said to Israel:

> The Lord said to Moses at Mount Sinai, "Speak to the Israelites and say to them: 'When you enter the land I am going to give you, the land itself must observe a Sabbath

to the Lord. For six years sow your fields, and for six years prune your vineyards and gather their crops. But in the seventh year the land is to have a year of Sabbath rest, a Sabbath to the Lord.' (Leviticus 25:1-4 NIV)

In other words, the Lord told the nation of Israel not to cultivate the land every seventh year. They were not to plant their lands or prune their vineyards every seventh year. This year was supposed to be set aside as a Sabbath year to the Lord, a year of rest dedicated to the Lord, a holy year. This was not the first time that Israel was told to do this. They were given the same commandment earlier during the Exodus:

Six years you shall sow your land and gather in its produce, but the seventh year you shall let it rest and lie fallow. (Exodus 23:10-11)

An important point to note here is that the Lord says what He means, and means what He says. The nation of Israel did not know this at the time, but God was going to hold them accountable for keeping this commandment on a national level. There was a practical reason the Lord told Israel to do this. During this seventh or Sabbath year the fields, vineyards and olive groves were open for the poor. This allowed the poor to gather all that they needed to sustain themselves. The land rested and the people rested. When the people of Israel did not keep this commandment, not only the poor suffered, but the nation as a whole suffered also. Seventy times this seventh Sabbath year came, and seventy times the nation of Israel failed to keep this special seventh year Sabbath. This special seventh Sabbath year was given a name—it was called the "Shemitah" year. Shemitah means "the release or the remission."

Prophecies that Intersect the Biblical Pattern

Now comes the time in the biblical pattern where the Shemitah year commandment intersects with the beastly kingdom pattern to modify the overall pattern. In fact, this is the time when we are given the details on four more of the beastly kingdoms. But let's see what happens before these enhancements of the pattern are given.

The capitol city of Jerusalem and the Jews were surrounded and ultimately defeated by the Babylonian King Nebuchadnezzar in 586 BC. The remaining Jews were carried off into Babylon and Israel ceased being a nation. They were now a composite of Israelites, primarily Jews, dominated by other nations that held power over them. So how did the Shemitah year commandment fully manifest within the Babylonian beastly kingdom prophecy? It enhanced the prophecy, and then modified it with the Lord holding the Jewish people accountable for their actions.

For seventy years the Israelites did not keep the Shemitah (Sabbath year) commandment voluntarily, but now they would keep the Shemitah years involuntarily in captivity to Babylon. The reason the Lord was doing this was described in Leviticus:

> I will turn your cities into ruins, and lay waste your sanctuaries…I myself will lay waste the land…Your land will be laid waste, and your cities will lie in ruins. Then the land will enjoy its Sabbath years all the time that it lies desolate and you are in the country of your enemies, then the land will rest and enjoy its Sabbaths. All the time that it lies desolate, the land will have the rest it did not have during the Sabbaths you lived in it. (Leviticus 26:31-35 NIV)

The land was going to have its rest that it did not have during the Sabbaths (Shemitah years) they lived in it. The Lord expected the Jewish people to do as he instructed them, but they rebelled against Him concerning the Shemitah years and many other things. The exact duration of their captivity was given in the Lord's Word also in two different places:

> This whole country will become a desolate wasteland, and these nations will serve the king of Babylon seventy years. (Jeremiah 25:11 NIV)

> The land enjoyed its Sabbath rests; all the time of its desolation it rested, until the seventy years were completed in fulfillment of the word of the Lord spoken by Jeremiah. (2 Chronicles 36:21 NIV)

What is interesting to note is that the commandment of the Shemitah year Sabbath prophecies fit completely within the Babylonian beastly kingdom pattern. The Jewish people were in captivity to the Babylonian Empire for the seventy years declared by the Lord, and then when the seventy years were complete, the judgment reserved for this beastly kingdom took place. This was the famous writing on the wall incident where the Babylonian King Belshazzar mocked God by using goblets taken from the Jewish temple and drank from them while they praised other gods. (Daniel chapter 5) The Babylonian Empire had run its course, the seventy years of captivity were fulfilled, and God would not be mocked by a Babylonian beastly kingdom that had caused so much destruction to His chosen people. The fact that the Babylonian Empire's time was up was decreed by the Lord in the following passage:

> "But when the seventy years are fulfilled, I will punish the king of Babylon and his nation, the land of the Babylonians for their guilt," declares the Lord, "and will make it desolate forever. I will bring on that land all the things I have spoken against it, all that are written...I will repay them according to their deeds and the work of their hands." (Jeremiah 25:12-14)

When it came time for the Babylonian Kingdom to fall, it happened in one night. The prophet Daniel told King Belshazzar that the Lord decreed his number was up, and the same night the Medo-Persian King Cyrus entered the city of Babylon and ended the Babylonian Empire. The biblical pattern held true once again. This time the culmination and end of a beastly empire coincided with the fulfillment of a prophecy that concluded at the same time. The prophecy of the seventy Shemitah years concluded, and the Babylonian Empire ended the same night. The preciseness of the biblical pattern is almost uncanny.

The Origin of the Beastly Kingdom Prophecies

It is important to note that it was within the time frame of the Babylonian Empire that the prophecy of the beastly kingdoms was given. The prophet Daniel described the great image in Nebuchadnezzar's dream and how this image was associated with the rise of four great empires. We are not going to spend time going over all the details of this image because countless others have given details that the reader can acquaint themselves with. There are some very important points that need to be made however. The kingdoms that arose were associated with metals and a beast counterpart as we are told in Daniel, chapter two and seven. Let's plot these out because these identifiers will be of critical importance later. Here are the beastly kingdoms with their metal identifiers and their animal designation counterpart:

Babylonian Empire	Gold	Lion with Eagles wings
Medo-Persian Empire	Silver	Bear
Grecian Empire	Bronze	Leopard
Roman Empire	Iron	No animal identifier given

There are some interesting points to be made from this list. Many of us forget that these ancient empires have an actual animal associated with them. The Babylonian Empire was associated with a Lion, the Medo-Persian Empire was linked with a Bear, and the Grecian Empire had a Leopard as an animal identifier. Then something curious happens with the Roman Empire. Daniel does not link this empire with any known animal; instead he describes the fourth beast in the following manner:

> After this I saw in the night visions, and behold a fourth beast, dreadful and terrible, and strong exceedingly; and it had great iron teeth: it devoured and brake in pieces, and stamped the residue with the feet of it: and it was diverse from all the beasts that were before it. (Daniel 7:7)

The fourth beast was described as being dreadful and terrible and exceedingly strong, but no animal was associated with it. Why was that? What was it about the Roman Empire that made it such an anomaly that no animal identifier was provided other than the somewhat nebulous "dreadful and terrible and exceedingly strong" description? It's almost as if the Roman Empire was something outside the normal beast empires parameters and an empire that would be separate and distinct from the other empires. What could the biblical pattern be hinting at?

From an exhaustive examination of the beastly empire biblical pattern, one fact will become very apparent. Any attempt to give the Roman Empire an animal identifier would detract from the proper unveiling of the seventh and eighth beastly kingdom empires. In fact, the Lion, Bear and Leopard identifiers will all be used in the description of the seventh and eighth beastly empires. Curiously missing is the Roman Empire beast. It's almost as if the Bible is trying to tell us not to focus on Roman Empire other than to use it to dig deeper and see what the biblical pattern is trying to tell us. We are going to have to go much deeper in our research of the Roman Empire to properly understand the gems of wisdom hidden here, because a casual examination of how this empire is different will not reveal all that the Lord wants us to know and may send us down a path where we fail to properly identify the mysterious seventh and eighth beast empires.

CHAPTER FOUR

Hidden Deep within the Roman Empire

If we are going to uncover how the Roman Empire is different, then we need to list the ways it is different from the other beast empires. When the prophet Daniel interpreted King Nebuchadnezzar's dream, he described a statue representing the different beastly kingdoms. The head of gold was the Babylonian Empire (Daniel 2:37-38), the chest and arms of silver was the Medo-Persian Empire (Daniel 8:20), the belly and thighs of bronze was the Grecian Empire (Daniel 8:21), and the legs of iron have been identified by Bible experts as the Roman Empire. This seems rather straight-forward but there is a critical difference with the Roman Empire. The Roman Empire was depicted as having two legs to stand on. It was not just one leg, but it was two legs. Why is this an important point?

In order to defeat the Roman Empire completely, you have to defeat not just one leg, but you have to be victorious over both legs of the empire. If only one leg is defeated, then you still have not fully conquered the entire Roman Empire. This is a critically important point in the proper identification of the beast empire that succeeded the Roman Empire. According to the biblical pattern we have established with the previous beast empires, the beastly kingdom that fully defeats the previous empire will be the next beastly kingdom to arise. Failure to properly follow this pattern will lead to false identification of the next beastly kingdom. We will examine in depth the next empire to arise in the next chapter. For now, it is important to note that the Roman Empire had two legs.

What is another way the Roman Empire was different from the others? The other beastly kingdoms had persecuted the Israelites and the Jews and were eventually destroyed because of their treatment of God's chosen people. During the time of the Roman Empire, Jesus Christ lived on earth and had His ministry. After Christ died on the cross, another group of people arose who chose Jesus Christ as their Savior. Now the Christians and Christianity would merit God's protection much like the Jews had. This was made clear by the Apostle Paul when he said that gentiles (non-Jews) would now be called the people of God:

> Even us, whom he also called, not only from the Jews but also from the Gentiles? As he says in Hosea, "I will call them my people who are not my people; and I will call her my loved one who is not my loved one. (Romans 9:24-25 NIV)

The Lord would now be protecting two different groups, the Jews and the Christians. Did the Roman Empire try to murder and kill both the Jews and the Christians? Absolutely! After Jesus Christ's death, the Jews revolted and were determined to throw off their Roman oppressors. This resulted in Rome sending four Roman legions to put down the rebellion. After much bloodshed and a prolonged siege, the Jewish people were defeated by the armies of Rome in 70 AD. Jerusalem was virtually destroyed as a city, their temple was demolished and the Jews were dispersed to different nations. This was the end of the Jews as a nation until their restitution to their land in 1948.

Were the other people of God, the Christians, murdered and killed by the Roman Empire also? Yes they were. Christians suffered severe persecution under Roman dominion from the time of the great fire in Rome in 64 AD until 313 AD when the Christian religion became legalized in Roman society. The most intense persecution came shortly after the time Rome burned. Christians were blamed and consequently were killed and murdered in countless numbers by the Roman Emperor Nero and others that succeeded him. Did the Roman Empire immediately meet its demise following its unbridled and wanton slaughter of both Jews and Christians? No it did not. What happened? What caused the delay in the biblical pattern yet again?

The biblical pattern was altered and modified by the Lord again by another prophecy that was given during the time of the Roman Empire and had to be fulfilled during the time the Roman Empire was in existence. It was another intersecting prophecy that would run its course when the beastly kingdom of the Roman Empire held dominion over the earth. What is remarkable about this prophecy was the fact that the day this prophecy was fulfilled was the exact day the next beast empire began its rampage across the earth. The biblical pattern would reassert itself yet again, and again, would anybody take notice and see what the Lord had done?

The fact that we are having this discussion means that the entire biblical pattern revealing the death and birth of various beastly kingdoms has been overlooked by the church today. The intersecting prophecy that altered and modified the destruction of the Roman Empire has not been recognized for what it is, and the church is almost totally ignorant of the true identity of the empire that will dominate the world scene during the turbulent last days before Christ's second coming. How did this happen? How could we as Christians miss something this important?

Rather than try to answer those questions, the more important course of action is to use all the resources and knowledge at our disposal to uncover the subtle clues that the Lord has given us to come to a proper understanding of what the Lord wants us to know in these times right now. Our survival and the survival of our families may depend on unlocking these crucial biblical patterns once and for all. The time of the end of our world as we know it today is rapidly approaching. A time of destruction awaits and the leader of a future beastly kingdom is ready to unleash devastation on the world. It's time we gain a proper understanding of just who this future leader might be.

We are going to discuss in detail the prophecy that intersected and modified the beastly kingdom prophecy, but before we do that there are some important points we need to make concerning what we have learned about the Roman Empire and its impact on the biblical pattern.

1. The Roman Empire is depicted as having two legs. What this means, from what we have learned from the biblical pattern, is that this

empire will not end when just one of the legs is defeated. The traditional Roman Empire's epicenter was the city of Rome. Most people think the Roman Empire ended when its last western emperor Romulus was defeated by the Germanic tribes under the leadership of German leader Odoacer in 476.[1] This is only partially true. The Roman Empire had a second leg, the Eastern Roman Empire set up by the Emperor Constantine. This was also known as the Roman Byzantine Empire and the eastern leg of the Roman Empire continued on for almost another thousand years until it was conquered in 1453.[2] This point is very crucial for the biblical pattern because the second leg of the Roman Empire did not fall until 1453.

2. A pattern of two emerges during the time of the Roman beastly kingdom. There were two legs that the empire stood upon, and there were two different groups of people that the Lord would now call his people—the Jews and the Christians. This does not mean that these two separate bodies of people would be immune from persecution, but now the Lord would look after both groups and shape their destinies. God was going to hold accountable those nations and peoples who killed and murdered His people, either Jews

---

1 UShistory.org, Ancient Civilizations/The Fall of the Roman Empire
2 Byzantine Empire-History: https://history.com/topics/ancient-middle-east/byzantine-empire

or Christians, and the Lord was going to do it His way. The Lord was going to accomplish this within His biblical patterns that He established, and it was all going to work out to fulfill His will in the time frame He set. We may not understand why things happened the way they did, but we can certainly learn from them. One of the ways we can learn is to take a closer look at this pattern of two that emerged during the Roman Empire.

The Pattern of Two and its Significance

We just discussed the two legs of the Roman Empire, and the two groups of people that the Lord would look after. Now there is something else we need to see. Take a look at the following pattern:

      1   2   [3 4 5 6]   7   8

What is the significance of this pattern? From just a simple observation we have two numbers, 1 and 2 that stand apart, then four numbers that are clustered together (3, 4, 5, and 6), and then two more numbers that stand apart from the pattern at the end (7 and 8). If we think about the beastly kingdoms, then it becomes apparent that they fit this pattern precisely. We had the Egyptian Empire (1) and the Assyrian Empire (2) standing apart, followed by the cluster of four beast empires that the prophet Daniel explained to us [Babylonian (3), Medo-Persian (4), Grecian (5), and Roman (6)] and then two more at the end, the yet to be revealed seventh (7) and eighth (8) beast empires. Let's recreate the pattern with the name of the empires we know:

Hidden Deep within the Roman Empire

Egyptian	Assyrian	[Babylonian	Medo-Persian	Grecian	Roman]	?	?
1	2	[3	4	5	6]	7	8

So why does this need to be pointed out? When we look for the prophecy that intersects and modifies the Roman Empire beastly kingdom pattern, it will be talking about and referring to the final two beastly kingdoms, the seventh and eighth beasts in this pattern. Just as there were two beastly kingdoms before the cluster of four in the Daniel prophecies, there will be two more following the cluster of four described by Daniel. They will be known as the seventh and eighth beastly kingdoms. It is now time to uncover just who the seventh beast kingdom is and the part it will have in the annals of history.

CHAPTER FIVE

The Seventh Beastly Kingdom

Going by the clues we have uncovered in the biblical pattern, there are certain things we should be looking for in our search for the seventh beastly kingdom. It will exhibit many of the same characteristics we have discovered in the previous six empires. It is absolutely critical that we describe some of the clues we have uncovered because the correct seventh beast empire will possess all of the identifiers of its predecessors. The seventh beastly kingdom will have the following characteristics:

1. It will appear on the world scene after conquering the second and final leg of the Roman Empire.
2. It will be identified by a prophecy given in scripture that becomes an intersecting pattern and will modify and alter the fate of the sixth beastly kingdom-the Roman Empire. This prophecy will establish the basis for the unveiling of the seventh beastly kingdom.

3. The seventh beastly kingdom will be depicted as a beast in prophecy and will be associated with the number seven since it is the seventh empire in the beastly kingdom prophecies.

4. We should look for components in the revealing prophecy that will associate this empire with identifiers of the previous beastly kingdoms.

5. The seventh empire will exhibit the same hatred and intolerance of not only Jews, but now Christians also—with the same zeal the previous beastly kingdoms had persecuted the Jews.

6. A subtle pattern of two will be evident in this empire.

7. There will be something that needs to happen in this seventh empire that will explain the delay in judgment of the Roman Empire. The Romans had murdered and killed countless numbers of Jews and Christians and yet did not meet their fate until hundreds of years later. There must be a reason for this delay.

8. The demise of the seventh beastly kingdom will lay the groundwork for the appearance of the eighth and final beastly kingdom.

It will be very difficult for any empire in previous world history to satisfy all of the components we have listed above. The only empire that fits the above pattern precisely is the empire we are going to discuss now. Not only does this empire meet all of the above qualifications, but it fits the pattern so specifically that it leaves little doubt that it is indeed the seventh beast empire. We will go over the pertinent points listed above so there can be little doubt of the authenticity of the seventh beast empire.

The Destroyer of the Roman Empire

Let's review the complete demise of the sixth beastly kingdom—the Roman Empire. Rome was conquered in two phases. In the traditional Roman Empire, the one centered in the city of Rome, a general decay had begun that led to the eventual destruction of the empire in this location. The Emperor Constantine was aware of the decline and split the Roman Empire into two locations. He moved the eastern leg of the Roman Empire to Turkey. The capital city of the eastern leg of the empire, called the Roman Byzantine Empire, was named Constantinople. All affairs of the eastern portion of the Roman Empire were concentrated in Constantinople, and it remained as a virtually impregnable fortress even after trouble began in the west around Rome.

The Roman Empire centered in Rome declined to the point where it was eventually conquered by hordes of Germanic tribesmen that descended on the empire by the hundreds of thousands. Their leader was named Odoacer and he completely sacked the city of Rome and took possession of it in 476.[3] The Western Roman Empire never recovered from this onslaught and never revived their former glory.

---

3   UShistory.org, Ancient Civilizations/the Fall of the Roman Empire

The Eastern Roman Empire centered in Constantinople was a different story. There were many that tried to conquer it but none were successful. It continued on for almost another thousand years until a particularly brutal leader arose that had the cunning and skill to breach the walls surrounding Constantinople and conquer the last remaining vestiges of the Roman Empire. He was the leader of the Islamic Caliphate and he came from the Ottoman Empire. His name was Mehmed II.[4]

Now we have the important missing clue on who conquered the last leg of the Roman Empire. It was a Muslim leader named Mehmed II, and he was the leader of the Ottoman Empire. Therefore, the Ottoman Empire and an Islamic Caliphate led by Mehmed II were the final conquerors of the Roman Empire. This also began a time when the leadership of the Muslim world (the Caliphate) moved to the Ottoman Empire where it would remain for hundreds of years.

We now have our missing clue to the identity of the seventh beastly kingdom. It points squarely at the Ottoman Empire, the Islamic religion, and the leadership of the Islamic religion known as the Caliphate.

The Prophecy, the Beast and the Animal Identifiers

Will the other points we outlined above point as clearly to the Ottoman Empire, the Islamic religion and the leadership of the Muslim world, the Caliphate, as the mysterious seventh beastly kingdom? Let's take a closer look.

---

4   Byzantine Empire-History: https://history.com/topics/ancient-middle-east/byzantine-empire

The Seventh Beastly Pattern

When we listed the characteristics of the seventh beastly kingdom, under points two, three and four, we said that we would be looking for a prophecy that depicts the seventh beastly kingdom, that the seventh beastly kingdom would be described as a beast in this prophecy, and that this kingdom would be linked to animal identifiers from previous beastly kingdoms. Does such a prophecy in God's Word exist?

Yes it does. It was given to the Apostle John from Jesus Christ Himself when John was exiled on the island of Patmos. The prophecy was given during the time the sixth beastly empire, the Roman Empire, was dominating the world. The prophecy is found in the Book of Revelation. Let's examine it now.

> And I stood upon the sand of the sea, and saw a beast rise up out of the sea, having seven heads and ten horns, and upon his horns ten crowns, and upon his heads the name of blasphemy. And the beast which I saw was like unto a leopard, and his feet were as the feet of a bear, and his mouth as the mouth of a lion: and the dragon gave him his power, and his seat, and great authority. (Revelation 13:1-2)

There are many points in this scripture that we need to interpret. The imagery of the sea is used twice in this passage. Biblical scholars have long pointed out that metaphorically the sea stands for the many people clustered around the Mediterranean Sea. The imagery of a beast is given; precisely what we said would be necessary to indicate that another beastly kingdom was arising. So, from the beginning parts of this passage we can conclude that this scripture is telling us another beastly kingdom is arising and it will come from people clustered by the Mediterranean Sea.

Next we have the depiction of the beast having seven heads. This is a strange depiction but it helps us to understand the descriptive imagery the Bible is using. The Bible is trying to tell us that the beast is representative of a system that is common to all the different heads. We learned from the first point in the biblical pattern that an Islamic Caliphate was responsible for the final destruction of the Roman Empire, and that this Islamic Caliphate was led by a leader of the Islamic system, the Ottoman Empire. The biblical pattern and this biblical verse are trying to tell us that this religious system (the Islamic Caliphate) is the beast arising out of the sea, and that one of the heads is the Ottoman Empire.

Is this the correct conclusion to make? Let's look at this more closely and see if our understanding of this passage is correct. There is a historical record of the Islamic religion that we can observe and verify. The Islamic or Muslim religion was established by the prophet Muhammad among different Arabic groups. After his death in 632 the Islamic religion needed a new leader and they appointed someone to be the religious successor to Muhammad. The new leader of the Islamic religion was called a caliph, which means successor, and those under the new leaders control were called the Caliphate. The Muslim religion was very successful and spread to many different countries and peoples. This includes most of the countries in Northern Africa, almost all of the Middle East, and many of the countries around the Black Sea and into the Balkans. Therefore imagery employed that said the beast (the

Islamic religion under control of the caliphate) arose out of many different people by the Mediterranean Sea would be entirely correct.

So if the beast depicted in Revelation chapter thirteen is correct (the Islamic Caliphate), then who are the seven different heads that this passage talks about? There is a fact that the western world is almost entirely unaware of, but is well known in the Islamic world. After the Prophet Muhammad's death, there were seven different Caliphate dynasties or heads that arose to lead the Muslim world. So that there can be no question about the seven different heads of the Islamic Caliphate, we are going to list them below with the time frame they ruled.

The Seven Heads of the Islamic Caliphate

1. The Rashidum Caliphate (632-661)
2. The Umayyad Caliphate (661-750)
3. The Abbasid Caliphate of Baghdad and Cairo (750-1258, 1261-1517)
4. The Fatimid Caliphate (909-1171)
5. The Umayyid of Cordoba Caliphate (929-1031)
6. The Almohad Caliphate (1147-1269)
7. The Ottoman Caliphate (1517-1924)[5]

These are the seven heads of the Islamic Caliphate. All of them at different times were the leadership of the Islamic religion. What is curious on this list is the fact that during some years there were two different leaders of the Islamic Caliphate.

---
5   Wikipedia, "Caliphate", https://en.wikipedia.org/wiki/caliphate

For example, during the years of 909-1171 you had both the Abbasid and Fatimid Caliphate, from 929-1031 you had the Abbasid and Umayyid Caliphate, and from 1147-1269 you had the Abbasid and Almohad Caliphate. That means that during three different times in the rule of the seven Caliphate dynasties you had two leaders. That makes a total of 10 leaders (7+3) during the rule of the Caliphate dynasties. What is very interesting is the fact that the descriptive prophecy (Revelation 13:1) referring to the seven heads of the beast says that the seven heads will have ten horns. A horn is used in the scriptures to depict a leader or king. (Revelation 17:12)

This is exactly the way the horns are portrayed in the verse we have been analyzing. The beast is depicted as having "seven heads and ten horns, and upon his horns ten crowns" which denotes kingship or leadership. This is an important point to remember. A horn is a leader or king in the scriptures. The fact that this beast arising from the sea has seven heads and ten horns fits the Islamic religion and the Islamic Caliphate exactly because the seven heads of the Islamic Caliphate had ten horns or leaders during this time matching the scripture in Revelation.

The Revelation thirteen prophecies also link the arising beast as having the animal identifiers associated with previous beast kingdoms. "And the beast which I saw was like unto a leopard, and his feet were as the feet of a bear, and his mouth as the mouth of a lion." (Revelation 13:2) Is the Islamic religion also linked with these former beast empires? As we have discussed before, the leopard was associated with the Grecian Empire, the bear with the Persian Empire, and the lion with the Babylonian Empire. If we look at a globe of the earth today, the areas controlled by the former Grecian Empire are predominately Islamic, the Persian Empire is almost entirely Islamic, and the Babylonian Empire which was centered in the modern nation of Iraq is almost completely Islamic also. All three of these animal identifiers are pointing toward a portion of the world that is almost entirely controlled by the Muslim Religion. Can there be any question what the biblical pattern and these verses are trying to show us?

This also brings up an important point on why the prophet Daniel never listed a known beast in association with the Roman Empire. The other three beastly kingdoms were all associated with a beast and an area that is now under Islamic control but the Roman Empire was not. If any beast had been linked with the Roman Empire we might be led to think that the new beast depicted as rising out of the sea would be associated with Rome and the new beastly kingdom also. In essence, it would be pointing us in the wrong direction. Instead, all of the beasts used as animal identifiers (leopard, bear and lion) are now clearly associated with the Islamic religion. This is a subtle way that the Lord is telling us that the traditional Roman Empire centered in the city of Rome is not part of the new beast empire rising out of many people and we should be looking at areas controlled by the nation of Islam and the Islamic Caliphate.

The Formation of the Seven Heads of the Islamic Caliphate

In many ways what we have identified as the seventh beast kingdom (the Ottoman Empire under control of an Islamic Caliphate) is contrary to what we have been taught. Yet it fits precisely with the biblical pattern. Will the other characteristics of the seventh beast kingdom fit as precisely? For example, why was there such a huge gap of time until the final fall of the Roman Empire centered in the eastern leg of the Roman Byzantine Empire? When we described the characteristics indicative of the seventh beastly kingdom, under point seven, we said that something needed to happen in the seventh beastly kingdom to explain the delay in judgment of the Roman Empire. After all, the Roman Empire had lasted from before the time of Christ until 1453 when an Islamic Caliphate under the direction of Mehmed II conquered the last vestiges of that empire. What needed to happen to cause this delay? If we scrutinize the formation of the seven heads of the Islamic Caliphate, then we can deduce the answer. The Islamic Empire needed a certain period of time for all seven heads of the Caliphate to form.

When the prophecy of the seventh beast rising out of the sea was given, the Islamic religion had not even been formed yet. The Muslim religion started with Muhammad and the Islamic Caliphate was formed after his death in 632. Then a certain period of time was needed for each head (Rashidun, Umayyads, Abbasids etc.) to reign and be replaced. It wasn't until the formation of the seventh head of the Caliphate, the Ottoman head, that the biblical pattern was ready to continue. When Mehmed II conquered Constantinople, the capitol city of the Roman Byzantine Empire in 1453, Rome was vanquished and the new seventh beastly kingdom rose from the ashes. The Ottoman Empire was the seventh of the Caliphate dynasties and the seventh beastly kingdom in the biblical pattern. It took time for all seven heads of the Islamic Caliphate to form, and when the time was right the biblical pattern reasserted itself. And all of this happened in 1453, with the fall of Rome and the rise of the Ottomans. This was just like the precedent set in the rise and fall of the previous beast empires—one fell and the almost immediately another took its place.

After the fall of Constantinople, Mehmed II moved his headquarters there and began the process of moving the Islamic Caliphate to the new location of Constantinople. Constantinople was eventually renamed Istanbul in 1930.

Now that we have seen how the Islamic Caliphate and the Ottoman empire meet the characteristics of the seventh beastly kingdom in the biblical pattern, it is now time to discover what else the prophecy in Revelation 13 has to say about the seventh head and its fate in end time prophecies. What we learn there is crucial for our understanding today.

CHAPTER SIX

The Fate of the Seventh Beastly Kingdom

The seventh beastly kingdom, the Ottoman Empire, had a fate that was set by the prophecies in Revelation. We are not told very much about this empire, but what we are told is very significant and highly prophetic. After telling us about the rise of the beast out of the sea, and the fact that it would have seven heads and would be composed of parts of other beast empires, the scripture in Revelation 13 goes on to tell us the fate of this seventh beast empire.

> And I saw one of the heads as it were wounded to death. (Revelation 13:3)

Let's unpack the meaning of this passage. First of all it mentions "one of the heads." What does that mean? We had previously listed the seven heads or dynasties of the Islamic Caliphate. The seventh head of the beastly empire was the Ottoman Empire, and the Ottoman Empire was the beastly empire referred to when the scripture says it would be wounded to death. That means that the Ottoman Empire was going to be discontinued as an empire or in other words killed. (Wounded to death) This passage is telling us that the Ottoman Empire was going to cease to exist. That brings up several questions: Did the Ottoman Empire cease to exist? How did that happen? And maybe most importantly, why did it happen?

In order to answer these questions let's review some history. The Ottoman Empire was officially ended by a leader in the nation of Turkey on March 3rd, 1924. The leader in Turkey that ended the Islamic Caliphate was Mustafa Kemal Ataturk.[6] This was a landmark event because the nation of Turkey had a history that was intertwined with the office of the Caliphate for almost 500 years. We need to remember that the Ottoman Caliphate almost conquered western civilization in the Middle Ages. The Ottomans had spread as far as Vienna, Austria in 1683 until they were finally turned back.[7] The Caliphate was synonymous with Turkey when it was a world empire and leadership from the Caliphate was integral to the success of the Ottoman Empire. To Muslims, one of the darkest days in Islamic history occurred when the seventh head of the Islamic Caliphate was dissolved in 1924. To the body of Muslim believers, the loss of the voice of Islam through the Caliphate was an inconsolable loss. They no longer had a united voice leading them. This was not the way it was supposed to be in the Islamic world and Turkey and the Turkish leader were partially to blame because they were the ones that abolished the Caliphate along with the Ottoman Empire. The beast was still alive (Islamic religion) but it had no head.

What were the factors that led to the demise of the Ottoman Empire and the office of the Caliphate? How did it happen?

---

6 Wikipedia, "The Ottoman Caliphate," http://en.wikipedia.org/w/index.php?title_Caliphate&oldid=653919004
7 Ibid

The Fate of the Seventh Beastly Kingdom

There is a two part answer to that question. One part involves the Jewish people and the Ottoman involvement in Jerusalem and the Jewish homeland set apart by God Himself, and the other involves the treatment of a minority Christian population by the Islamic Ottoman Empire.

Here's what happened. The Ottoman Empire was tremendously successful in conquering different countries. Not only had they penetrated deep into the heart of Europe, but they also occupied the city of Jerusalem and controlled the entire Jewish homeland. They were so successful in dominating the region around Jerusalem that they began to boast that they would never give up the Jewish Holy Land and would never relinquish control of Jerusalem. In fact, they said it was impossible for them to ever leave this area. The Ottomans were so convinced that this would never happen that they had a self-proclaimed prophecy concerning the area around Jerusalem. Here are the words of that prophecy:

> When the waters of the Nile flow into Palestine, then will a prophet of the Lord come and drive the Turks out of this land.[8]

The Turks and the Ottoman Empire were doubly sure that this saying could never take place because it was impossible for the Nile River to flow miles and miles across the Sinai Desert into Palestine by Jerusalem, and all the prophets of God had died hundreds of years before their time. This saying had held true for countless centuries, and the Turks were convinced

---

8   Into All Truth, "As Birds Flying: Jerusalem 1917," Into All Truth Ministries, http://www.nccg.org/iat/birds.html

that the sword of Islam would always hold sway over the area around Jerusalem.

The problem was that the Ottoman Empire under the Turks had placed themselves in direct opposition to the will of the Lord. God had said that Jerusalem and the lands around it belonged to the nation of Israel. Nothing the Turks ever did would prevent the land from returning to the Jews when the Lord determined it was time. God began to work behind the scenes to accomplish His purpose.

A man was sent by British forces to free the Jewish homeland and the city of Jerusalem from Islamic Ottoman domination in World War I. His name was Edmund Allenby and he was a general placed in charge of British, Australian and New Zealand armed forces. On October 31st, 1917, he put his plan for the recapture of the city of Jerusalem into action. One of the problems plaguing his troops was the lack of water in this area. To solve the problem, General Allenby had his engineers tap into the Nile River and run a pipeline that followed the advance of his army right into Palestine near Jerusalem. With the pipeline in place, his troops had access to thousands of gallons of water a day that came directly from the Nile River. When General Allenby and his forces reached the gates of Jerusalem, he had airplanes drop leaflets with his name on them telling the Ottoman Turkish forces inside Jerusalem that if they left immediately they would not be fired upon. Miraculously, all Turkish Ottoman troops fled Jerusalem the night of December 8th, 1917, and by December 9th they were all gone. According to God's will, General Allenby had accomplished the impossible and captured the city of Jerusalem without a shot being fired inside the gates of Jerusalem.

The Fate of the Seventh Beastly Kingdom

When the Ottoman forces were questioned about their frantic departure from Jerusalem, it became apparent that they were absolutely terrified of General Allenby. In Arabic, the name Allenby translates into "Allah-en-Nebi" which means "Prophet of God." To the Turkish Ottoman Muslims, a man named "the prophet of God" brought the waters of the Nile into Palestine near Jerusalem and ended an occupation that had lasted many centuries. They left because the impossible prophecy had been fulfilled. The Ottoman Empire had gone against the will of God, and was soundly defeated because of its actions.

This action of the Ottomans against the Jews led to their downfall. This was not the only thing the Ottomans did that paved the way for their ruin. While it's true that Turkey had aligned itself with Germany in WWI, and that was a contributing factor, there is another crucial event that has often been overlooked in history that was critical to the disintegration of the Ottoman Empire. This was an insidious event that is scarcely acknowledged to this day and is barely talked about in world history. This event was an act of genocide. The Turkish Ottoman Empire targeted a Christian minority population for extermination.

The tragedy began on April 24th, 1915, when the government of Turkey and the religious office of the Caliphate declared "Jihad" on the Armenian Christian population living in their land. The Armenian Christians had formed the first independent Christian nation in the world with millions of people living in their country for centuries until they were absorbed by the Ottoman Empire. Then on April 24th, 1915, the Ottoman Empire decided this peaceful Christian group was a threat to their empire and systematically rounded up all the Christian leaders and intellectuals and killed them. The Ottomans began a campaign of extermination that targeted every Christian they could find. Some Armenian Christians were herded into the mountains and killed, while others were forced to march into the deserts on endless walks without food or water until they died. When this holocaust ended, over one and a half million Armenian Christians had lost their lives.[9]

The Ottoman Empire had endured for centuries until they committed this unspeakably brutal act against the Christian population living within their borders. The Lord holds nations accountable for their actions and the Ottoman Empire had placed the final nail in their own coffin. The collapse of the Ottoman Empire began and it was finished by the work of another man that succeeded against almost impossible odds. Not everyone in the Islamic world was pleased with the leadership of the Islamic Caliphate coming out of the Ottoman Empire centered in Istanbul.

A strange coalition began to form in the Muslim world. One of the disaffected Islamic groups was the house of Saud, located in what now is the nation of Saudi Arabia. They are better known as the Saudis and they began to view the Ottoman Caliphates as a corrupt group of old men that were mostly concerned with amassing wealth and harems of beautiful women. They were joined by a powerful Arabian tribe known as the Hashemites who shared those same views. The Hashemites include many of the ruling families of the present day nations of Iraq, Syria and Jordan.[10] Both the Saudis and the Hashemites began to despise the Ottoman Caliphates and were determined to do something to bring down the ruling Ottomans. (We need to take note of these three groups [Saudis, Hashemites and

---

9 Glen Beck, "It is About Islam," (New York, NY: Threshold Editions/Mercury Radio Arts, 2015), P. 53
10 Wikipedia, "Hashemites," https://en.wikipedia.org/wiki/Hashemites

The Fate of the Seventh Beastly Kingdom

Ottomans] in this strange coalition because they will form the foundation in another biblical pattern we will discuss later.)

Into this boiling cauldron of competing agendas and unbridled ambition to rule the Islamic world stepped an opportunistic young leader with a different goal in mind. This leader was appointed by the nation of Britain and given the specific task of fomenting a rebellion among the differing Islamic groups against the Ottoman Empire. This leader's name was T. E. Lawrence. He is better known to us today as "Lawrence of Arabia." Because of his dashing leadership, and the might of the Saudi and Hashemite armies supporting him, Lawrence of Arabia was able to defeat the Ottomans and seize control over much of the Middle East. This enabled the nations of the world to set up the current boundaries of the nations in this area after WWI.

The Ottoman Empire was crumbling apart with their military might virtually destroyed by the end of WWI. The last vestiges of the religious arm of the Ottomans, the Caliphate, held on until it was finally disbanded by the new ruler in Turkey. His name was Mustafa Kemal Ataturk and he effectively killed the Ottoman Empire when he ended the Caliphate on March 3rd, 1924.[11]

The Ottoman Empire was no more. The seventh head of the Islamic ruling dynasties and the seventh head of the beast rising up out of the sea were wounded to death. In its wake, the Ottoman Empire left a legacy of destruction that spanned several centuries. In light of what we have been discussing in the biblical pattern, this leaves a rather perplexing dilemma. The previous beastly kingdom was always replaced by the

---

[11] Wikipedia, "The Ottoman Caliphate," http://en.wikipedia.org/w/index.php?title_Caliphate&oldid=653919004

entity that defeated it. In this case, the Ottoman Empire and the Islamic Caliphate was ended and disbanded by a leader from the nation of Turkey. For the biblical pattern to hold true, a future leader from the nation of Turkey must be the leader that starts or revives the new beastly kingdom that will become the eighth and last beastly kingdom. For the biblical pattern to remain consistent, this is what must happen. Could this highly unlikely scenario possibly be the framework that paves the way for the appearance of the eighth beast kingdom? Before we discuss the appearance of the eighth beast empire, let's summarize what we have discovered about the seventh beastly kingdom, the Ottoman Empire:

- The Ottoman Empire was the empire that finally defeated the Roman Empire in 1453 when Mehmed II sacked the city of Constantinople. Soon afterward, Constantinople became the new headquarters of the Islamic Caliphate and was eventually renamed Istanbul.
- The Ottoman Empire became the seventh beast empire in the biblical pattern.
- The Islamic Caliphate was an integral part of the ruling head of the Ottoman Empire.
- The Ottoman Empire dominated vast portions of the world for almost 500 years.
- The Ottomans almost conquered the western world until they were stopped in the heart of Europe in 1683.
- The seventh beastly kingdom, the Ottoman Empire, claimed Jerusalem and the surrounding

land as their land in direct opposition to what God has decreed. The Ottoman Turks were removed from Jerusalem after occupying it for hundreds of years by General Allenby in 1917.

- The Islamic Caliphate led by the Ottomans committed genocide against the Armenian Christian population in 1915 which led to the deaths of a million or more Armenians.
- The Ottoman Empire was ended by a leader from the nation of Turkey.
- The Islamic Caliphate and the last vestiges of the Ottoman Empire ended on March 3rd, 1924.

Now that we have laid the groundwork for the seventh beastly kingdom, let's turn our attention to the eighth beastly kingdom and see what the passages in the Bible have to say about this mysterious entity.

CHAPTER SEVEN

The Rise of the Eighth Beast Empire

The seventh beast empire ended on March 3rd, 1924 when Mustafa Kemal Ataturk of Turkey disbanded the Islamic Caliphate and with it the last vestiges of the Ottoman Empire. What has happened since that time? The Islamic world has been leaderless without the Caliphate to direct them. This loss has been deeply felt by the entire Muslim world. They have become a world of competing factions driven by their own agendas and constantly at odds with each other.

The schism in the Islamic nations has become more pronounced in recent years. They have fractured into two separate groups, each struggling for control and insisting that they have the right to lead all of Islam. The largest group is known as the Sunni Muslims, and they comprise the vast majority of Muslim nations. The smaller group is known as the Shiite Muslims and they are clustered primarily in the nation of Iran. We will discuss them in depth later but the important thing to note is that both of these groups feel that they should be the ones that lead the Muslim nations. Both are waiting for a time when a strong leader rises up to lead all of Islam. What both of these groups have failed to notice is that the Bible discusses a time when just such a strong leader emerges, and he will arise exactly the way the biblical pattern has shown us.

When we discuss the emergence of the eighth beast empire, the best way we can approach this is from what God's Word has to say about this subject. We need to look at the clues we have been given and apply what we have learned from the biblical pattern. We need to go back to the passages in the Bible that describe the seventh beast empire, and see what they have to say about the eighth beast empire. Let's take a look at those passages now.

> And I saw one of his heads as it were wounded to death; and his deadly wound was healed. (Revelation 13:2)

Let's discern the meaning of this before we move on. We have already discussed how the head that was wounded to death represented the Ottoman Empire and the Islamic Caliphate. Now this passage in Revelation is telling us that the wound is going to be healed. What does that mean? It would appear that God's Word is telling us that the Ottoman Empire is going to be revived and is going to be reinstated as a controlling power on the earth. It is going to be "healed" or restored to its power. Let's contemplate the implications of what this passage is telling us and what that means will happen in our world.

The Ottoman Empire ruled from the nation of Turkey. It was headquartered in the nation of Turkey and it was ruled from Istanbul which is the main city in the nation of Turkey. An integral part of this ruling head was the Islamic Caliphate, which means that the Islamic Caliphate is going to be restored to the nation of Turkey also. Are you noticing a pattern here?

The Rise of the Eighth Beast Empire

The modern day nation of Turkey is a key component in the restoration of the Ottoman Empire. The nation of Turkey has been a major player in world politics in the past, and will be a major player in the world political scene in the future. With so much emphasis placed on the nation of Turkey and its reemergence in the forefront of global politics as the eighth beastly kingdom, is there any other place in God's Word that speaks of the demise and restoration of the seventh beast, and how that beast will become the eighth beast in this series of beastly kingdoms?

Indeed there is. It is found in the Book of Revelation.

> And there are seven kings: five are fallen, and one is, and the other is not yet come; and when he cometh he must continue a short space. And the beast that was, and is not, even he is the eighth, and is of the seven, and goeth into perdition. (Revelation 17:10-11)

If we look carefully at this passage, and remember it was the Apostle John that was giving us this information, then we can see that John is reciting the occurrence of the beastly kingdoms and how they will play out. John tells us there are seven kings and that five are fallen. In John's day, the five beasts that had fallen were the Egyptian, Assyrian, Babylonian, Medo-Persian, and Grecian empires. The one that was in his time was the Roman Empire, and then John refers to a beast that is not yet come. This was the Ottoman Empire, the seventh. John then states that this beast must continue a short space. In the case of the original Ottoman Empire, it continued for about 500 years.

John then goes on to say that the beast that was (Ottoman Empire), and is not (the Ottoman Empire ended on March 3rd,

1924), even he (Ottoman Empire) is the eighth (the renewed Ottoman Empire), and is of the seven (the old Ottoman Empire.)

In essence, John is telling us the same thing we found in Revelation 13:3 that the old Ottoman Empire based in Turkey was going to be gone, but would reappear on the world scene and would become the eighth beastly kingdom, the renewed Ottoman Empire. There are two different places in God's Word that are telling us exactly the same thing: the Ottoman Empire in Turkey is going to die, but then will be renewed and will reemerge at the eighth beastly kingdom empire.

What else do the passages say about the leader that will emerge to lead this new beastly kingdom? Let's see.

> And they worshipped the dragon which gave power unto the beast: and they worshipped the beast, saying, Who is like unto the beast? Who is able to make war with him? (Revelation 13:4)

The new leader controlling the beastly empire is going to be so intrinsically associated with the eighth beastly empire that he himself is going to be called the beast. He is going to be controlled and given power by Satan who is personified as the dragon in this passage. The new leader personifies the beastly empire to the point the he becomes a beast himself.

Let's pause for a moment to consider the implications of what we are being told about the beastly kingdom and the leader that will soon emerge on the world scene. We need to put this in the perspective of what we know is happening in today's world.

The Current Situation in the Nation of Turkey

As of this time, has a renewed Ottoman Empire appeared in the nation of Turkey? No it has not. Currently in the nation of Turkey there is a profoundly unsettled situation. Turkey, until recently had been a democratic republic with many voices in its ruling government. That all changed when a new leader emerged on the political scene. He is a leader that is brutally egocentric, with no tolerance for opposing points of view. And he is the only leader in the world today who is emphatically calling for a restoration of the Ottoman Empire. A renewed Ottoman Empire is what this leader is clamoring for, and he is willing to put all of the resources in the nation of Turkey to work in order to achieve this goal. Who is this leader?

His name is Recep Tayyip Erdogan and he is currently the President of the nation of Turkey. Although he was born in Istanbul, he lived as a child in the city of Rize in the Gomer region of Turkey.[12] The Gomer region of Turkey is surrounded by the Magog, Meshech, Tubal and Togarmah regions of Turkey. (We will talk about this in depth later.) Perhaps we can see this best when we look at a map of ancient Turkey.

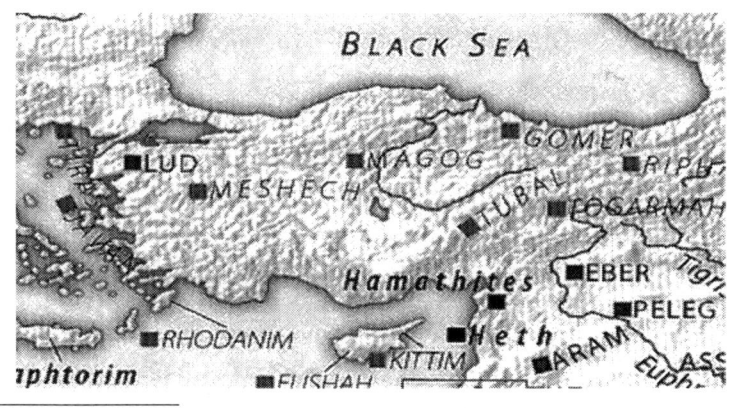

12 Wikipedia, Recep Tayyip Erdogan, https://en.wikipedia.org/wiki/Recep_Tayyip_Erdo%c4%9Fan

This map is from the *Moody Atlas of Bible Lands*, one of the best resources available to us in determining ancient locations. The city of Rize, the childhood home of President Erdogan, is on the Black Sea right above the letter R in Gomer, although it is not pictured on this map. Why are these ancient names of locations in Turkey being used in association with President Erdogan? Because these names are highly significant in biblical prophecy and a key identifier of a notorious character that will arise in times of turmoil in the future. These strange sounding names are both a geographical location and a namesake. For example, Magog was one of the sons of Japheth, a son of Noah, and denotes the name of a people and where they came to reside. You can see the Magog area clearly on the *Moody Atlas of Bible Lands*. Meshech and Tubal were sons of Japheth also and you can see that they are included on the map and the area in which they resided. All of these locations are clearly in the current day nation of Turkey.

The *Moody Atlas of Bible Lands* is not the only source that places Meshech, Tubal, Magog, Gomer and Togarmah firmly in ancient Turkey. Some of the most prestigious Bible reference books, such as the *Macmillan Bible Atlas* and the *Oxford Bible Atlas* also place these five entities in Turkey.

So we have a leader in Turkey who is using everything in his power to reestablish the Ottoman Empire, and he just happens to have connections to biblical areas that God's Word says will be of paramount importance in end time events. What else do we know about Recep Tayyip Erdogan?

In 2011, Mr. Erdogan ordered the Statue of Humanity torn down.[13] This was a monument dedicated to healing the rift between the

---

13   Ibid

Armenian Christian population and the Turkish people. Erdogan has become an adamant Armenian Holocaust denier.

Recep Tayyip Erdogan was elected the 12th president of Turkey on August 28th, 2014. Since his inauguration he has assumed almost dictatorial powers and has shut down almost all forms of opposition to his presidency. On July 15th, 2016, President Erdogan survived a coup d'état attempt by the military.[14] After this attempt, 200 journalists were arrested, 120 media outlets were closed, 50,000 people were arrested, 160,000 people were fired from their jobs, and tens of thousands of people were jailed on charges of terrorism.[15] Almost all forms of dissent to his presidency have been outlawed and his efforts to renew the Ottoman tradition in Turkey have increased.

When President Erdogan greeted President Mahmoud Abbas at his presidential palace, he met him with guards dressed in military garb depicting sixteen Turkish Empires in history.[16]

---

14 Ibid
15 Ibid
16 Cumhurbaskanligi@tccb.gov.tr
"T.C.Cumhurbaskanligi:CUMHURBASKANLIGI:tccb.gov.tr.

Using Biblical Patterns To Unlock End Time Events

After the coup attempt on July 16th, 2016, President Erdogan erected a monument that he said was to commemorate the coup attempt victims. It was unveiled on July 16th, 2017, but instead of honoring the victims, the monument was filled with symbolism that depicted the Ottoman Empire reemerging on the world stage. When President Erdogan unveiled the monument, he was surrounded by soldiers dressed as warriors from the old Ottoman Empire.

This picture is more like an image of a beast empire that President Erdogan wants to resurrect. For example, this monument contains the image of seven lifting up the crescent moon

The Rise of the Eighth Beast Empire

with a star in the middle of the horns of the moon. The seven lifting up the crescent moon represent the seven regions of Turkey. These regions are the Marmara, Black Sea, Eastern Anatolia, Southeast Anatolia, Central Anatolia, Mediterranean and Aegean regions. The curved crescent moon looks like two horns and is symbolic of the Ottoman Islamic Empire. The star is symbolic of a leader in the Islamic world that unites the entire Muslim world. At the base of the monument is the "Rub el Hizb," a two squared star in the Islamic world and within the star is the symbol of a dragon.

The eight sided star has always had Islamic connections and the dragon has long been a symbol for the devil. There are critical biblical codes here also that we will discuss later. All of these symbols are present in the new monument that President Erdogan erected in Turkey.[17] This is a symbol he said was dedicated to those who died in the coup of 2016, and yet it symbolizes intense imagery of a rising Ottoman Empire that intends to take over the Islamic world, the then the world in general. What is equally disturbing is the fact that the biblical pattern

---

17 Walid Shoebat, "Erdogan of Turkey Literally Resurrects the Image of the Ottoman Beast and Vows That All Who Defy Him will be Beheaded," http://shoebat.com/2017/07/18/erdogan-of-turkey-resurrects-the-image-of-the-beast-and-vows-that-all-who-defy-him-will-be-beheaded.

points out that a modern day leader in the nation of Turkey is the one that will bring back the Ottoman Empire, and when that happens the office of the Islamic Caliphate will come home to Turkey where it had been for almost five hundred years.

There is no other leader except Recep Tayyip Erdogan of Turkey who is trying to make this happen.

Will he succeed? Can he make this happen? Will the nation of Turkey bring back the Ottoman Empire and become the eighth beast kingdom depicted in prophecy? Is there anything hidden in the biblical pattern that might suggest when this might happen or a time frame we should be looking for?

While we may not be able to answer all of these questions, perhaps we can gain some insight that will help us. There can be little doubt we are living in the days of the formation of the eighth beast empire. It has not arrived yet but will soon be here. The clues to the arrival of the eighth beast empire may not be obvious to us now because we have not discovered all we need to see. Unrevealed to us up to this point in time, there is a prototype pattern concealed within the overall biblical pattern of the beastly kingdoms that will give us crucial clues we need to know. This prototype or shadow pattern will be a forerunner or type of things to come when the eighth beastly kingdom appears. The clues to the arrival of the eighth beast empire are revealed in the past in a prototype pattern we have not examined yet. Let's take a look at that shadow pattern now.

CHAPTER EIGHT

The Prototype Pattern for Revealing the Eighth Beast Empire

What do we mean when we talk about a prototype pattern? A prototype pattern is a precursor pattern that contains many of the elements we will see in the primary pattern. In other words it is a shadow pattern or a type of things to come. How do we determine the validity of a prototype pattern? We need to examine the prototype pattern and see if it contains similar elements found in the original pattern. For example: in the original beastly empire pattern, we looked for an entity that defeated the Roman Empire. This was a key element and a determining factor in the succession of the beast empires. Are there any other entities associated with the downfall of the Roman Empire? If there are, then studying that prototype entity will provide us with crucial clues needed to understand what we can expect with the advent of the coming eighth beast empire.

If we go back and review the information on the downfall of the western or original Roman Empire, a startling fact jumps out at us. There was another entity responsible for the downfall of the Roman Empire. The entity was the Germanic people, under the leadership of a German King. That German leader was Odoacer and he conquered the traditional Western Roman Empire in 476. So now we have an entity we can focus on—the German people. For this prototype pattern to be complete we must have a German leader that arose to lead the Germanic people. This leader must be compelling in his leadership style and so beast like in his ruthlessness in dealing with his fellow human beings that he seems to be the very embodiment of evil itself. In fact, in order for this leader to fit the prototype beast like pattern, he must exhibit the following characteristics found in the beastly kingdom pattern:

- He must rise to lead the German people.
- He will be trying to reassert a German Empire that was prematurely defeated in a previous war. (WW1)
- This leader will have spell-binding oratory skills that drive the German people to action.
- He will have a profound hatred for the Jews or any other chosen people that stand in the way of his master-race ideology.
- He will embrace things that are anti-God or occult-like in nature.
- He will possess antichrist like characteristics.
- The emerging leader will be profoundly militaristic and will want to take over the entire world.
- He will be beast like in his actions and treatment of others.

The Prototype Pattern for Revealing the Eighth Beast Empire

- Key dates and timings of things in his life will coincide with key dates in the emergence of the eighth beast empire.
- Key ideas from the prototype leader will be found in the emerging eighth beast empire.

There can be little doubt about which German leader fits all of these characteristics. Adolf Hitler fits every detail listed above. He was the personification of evil and his Third Reich fits every detail we could list as a prototype beast empire. His reign of terror and destruction is well known.

Adolf Hitler rose from relative obscurity to lead the German people. One of his most powerful tools was his speaking style. He began his speeches speaking softly and then slowly began to increase his volume and the intensity of his message. Hitler often spoke of the offences committed against Germany with the end of World War I and the unjust Versailles Treaty that demanded reparations from Germany. He would galvanize the crowd with his oratory skills and work them up into a fevered frenzy. He seized control of the German government and made it illegal to oppose him. Hitler built a military machine that was almost unstoppable and unleashed that military might upon the world.

Hitler found a scapegoat to blame all of Germany's problems on—the Jewish people. His "final solution" resulted in the deaths of six million Jews. He believed his Aryan ancestry was supposed to be the master race—not the Jews who were God's chosen people. His inspiration came from the occult and satanically enthused ideas. His misdeeds were legend, his propensity for inhumanity toward his fellow man was unbridled, and the darkness he unleashed upon the world was almost too much to be endured.

Hitler exuded so many antichrist like characteristics that it is hard to believe he would not be associated with the coming antichrist in some way. The Apostle John said in his writings that in the last days the antichrist would come, but before him there would be many antichrists.

> Little children, it is the last time: and as ye have heard that antichrist shall come, even now are there many antichrists; whereby we know that it is the last time. (1 John 2:18)

Adolf Hitler would qualify as one of these antichrists. What is relatively unknown is the fact that he qualifies as the prototype antichrist, a prelude to the actual antichrist, in a much more specific way. Let's take a look at the following virtually unknown facts.

In the Hebrew and Greek languages, each individual letter of the alphabet has a particular numeric value. When you have a completed word in the Hebrew language you can assign a numeric value to that word. The study of the numeric value of words is a unique branch of science known as "gematria." The science of gematria was well known in the time of John the Apostle and was used by cabbalistic Jews to interpret the deeper meanings hidden within the Torah. The Apostle John used gematria extensively when he recorded the message from Jesus Christ in the Book of Revelation.

The Prototype Pattern for Revealing the Eighth Beast Empire

One of the most well know examples of this is when John said that the beast that will arise in the end times is associated with a particular number—and the number of the beast is 666.

> Here is wisdom. Let him that hath understanding count the number of the beast: for it is the number of a man; and his number is Six hundred, threescore and six. (Revelation 13:18)

Somehow the coming beast mentioned in the Book of Revelation is going to be associated with the number 666. We don't know how, but in some manner the beast of Revelation will be linked synonymously with the number 666.

A group of researchers studying gematria in the Bible made a rather startling discovery when they started analyzing Nazi Germany and began tabulating the Hebrew numeric values of letters in names of different players involved in the Nazi regime. They took the name of Adolf Hitler and linked his name with the place of his birth—Austria and then tabulated the results. They were completely astonished when the computer presented the results of this analysis. The number the computer gave them was based on the numeric values of the Hebrew letters included in the names and totaled 666. They double checked the analysis to confirm the results and saw for themselves the unmistakable result:

Adolf= 121
Hitler= 254
Austria= 291
Total= 666[18]

---

[18] Gerard Bodson, *Cracking the Apocalypse Code*, (Element Books, Boston, MA 2000), P. 29

These findings would definitely qualify Adolf Hitler as a prototype of the coming antichrist in Revelation since his name and birthplace are associated with the 666 number. What else have we been missing in the prototype Hitler antichrist pattern? Are there any connections from Hitler's life that may provide important timing clues for the reappearance of the new Ottoman Empire, the eighth beast empire from the biblical pattern?

The First Timing Clue

Adolf Hitler would never have amounted to much if not for the pain and suffering he endured during WWI. It was a pivotal event in his life. The First World War was the event that shaped many of his ideas and molded the warped philosophies that became his life. With the First World War becoming such a turning point for Hitler, what was the pivotal date that started this monstrous conflict between nations?

The critical date for the start of the First World War was on June 28th, 1914 when Archduke Franz Ferdinand of Austria was assassinated. The seeds of war were sown on that date and without that event war would probably never have spread across the world and Hitler most likely would have remained a relative nobody. What if history repeated itself and a mirror like war pattern reestablished itself one hundred years later in June of 2014? Would that be a significant event and something that we should take note of?

Something did happen in June of 2014, almost on the same day that one hundred years earlier had started the cataclysmic events that would set the world on fire. A relatively unknown Muslim Cleric named Ibrahim Awad Ibrahim al-Badri stepped

The Prototype Pattern for Revealing the Eighth Beast Empire

forward and announced something apocalyptic. He is not known by his given name to most people. The name he chose for himself and the name he is known by is Abu Bakr al-Baghdadi and he is the self-appointed leader of ISIS. The pivotal event he announced on June 29th, 2014 was the reformation of the Caliphate, the governing body of the Islamic Religion. With this action, Abu Bakr al-Baghdadi had just resurrected the beast of Revelation 13 and the nations of the world barely noticed the significance of this world altering event. The beast that had been put to death in 1924, was alive again and ready to make war with Christ's chosen people—the Jews and the Christians. Not only was the world unaware of this pivotal event—but they were unprepared for what would soon be unleashed and the apocalyptic consequences of his actions.

After restoring the Caliphate, Abu Bakr al-Baghdadi promptly declared war on the entire world. In one of his opening addresses to the world, Abu Bakr said that the Islamic religion was not a religion of peace. "O Muslims, Islam was never for a day the religion of peace. Islam is the religion of war."[19] While Islam may be a religion of peace to some, to those taking control of the Caliphate it is anything but a religion of peace. As the new leader of the Caliphate, Abu Bakr began killing any people that did not agree with him. He set the pattern that all that controlled the newly formed Caliphate would follow—death and destruction to any who oppose them.

The only problem was that Abu Bakr al-Baghdadi was not the proper leader or head depicted in the biblical pattern. He resurrected the beast, but he would not be the one to control

---

19   Robert Spencer, "Islamic State Caliph: Islam is the Religion of War," Jihad Watch, May 14, 2015, http://www.jihadwatch.org/2015/05/islamic-state-caliph-islam-is-the-religion-of-war.

it. Turkey was the place where the real Caliphate and head would arise from. You cannot declare yourself the proper leader of the Caliphate, but this is what Abu Bakr al-Baghdadi tried to do. He raised the beast from the dead (Islam under the direction of the Caliphate) and under the guise of ISIS he has decimated the nations of Syria and Iraq. His minions have killed thousands of people in hideous ways in foreign countries including the United States. But try as he may, Abu Bakr al-Baghdadi was never going to be the leader that revived the eighth beast empire. He was destined for failure in that regard. Consequently, as of this time, he has faded almost into oblivion. The primary thing he managed to do was spread terrorism throughout the world and start wars in several nations. And he just happened to reinstate the Caliphate and start a war pattern almost 100 years to the day from the time the war pattern started in 1914. The beast was resurrected and spreading wars but it did not have the proper head.

Let's turn our attention back to Hitler and search for other times that had an impact in his life.

The Second Pivotal Time in Hitler's Life

Do any other times in Adolf Hitler's life have ties to the rise of the eighth beast empire? The First World War made him what he was, but a second pivotal time set him on a path that would define the rest of his life. There was a time in Hitler's life when he stood trial for treason against Germany, went to jail after being convicted of that crime, served his time in prison, finished his pivotal book *Mein Kamph* (My Struggle), and was released from prison to begin his eventual overthrow and takeover of the German government. All of these things

The Prototype Pattern for Revealing the Eighth Beast Empire

happened in the same year, 1924.[20] This was one of the most critical times in Hitler's life.

Is there anything else that happened of significance in 1924? In the same week that Hitler's trial for treason began, Mustafa Kemal Ataturk of Turkey disbanded the Islamic Caliphate, the head wound and death of the old Ottoman Empire. (Hitler's trial began on February 26th, 1924,[21] and Ataturk disbanded the Caliphate on March 3rd, 1924). This was a defining time in Hitler's life because the time in 1924 helped him clarify his ideas, encapsulate them in a book, and begin the path he would embark on to become an antichrist like leader.

We have seen history repeat in one hundred year patterns before. The curious ties between President Lincoln and Kennedy are examples of this. We just discussed a war pattern beginning in June of 1914 and reasserting itself in June of 2014. Could the reestablishment of the Ottoman Empire follow this same one hundred year pattern? While only our Heavenly Father knows for sure, there are some indicators that point to a pivotal date in the near future that we should be aware of. The primary indicator comes from the man who is the driving force for the reestablishment of the Ottoman Empire, Recep Tayyip Erdogan.

There is a tantalizing and highly significant fact that is virtually unknown to us in the west. President Erdogan of Turkey has set a goal for the reestablishment of the Ottoman Empire and moving the recently reestablished Islamic Caliphate back to Turkey. He wants the framework and everything in place

---

20   Leonard Mosley, *The Reich Marshal, A Biography of Herman Goring*, (Doubleday and Company, Garden City, NY 1974) P. 101
21   Ibid

by 2023 so he can resurrect the Ottoman Empire by March 3rd, 2024, the one hundred year anniversary of its death. He announced this to the world in the speech he gave on July 18th, 2017 when he unveiled his monument to the Ottoman Empire on the anniversary of the coup attempt against him. President Erdogan said this:

> We will reach our goals for 2023 with our people and no one will discourage us from achieving this neither the traitors of the Gulen organization, the PKK, nor allies who are working to encircle us along our borders.[22]

If we are carefully looking for a timing pattern for the resurrection of the Ottoman Empire then we have found it. March 3rd, 2024 is exactly one hundred years after the death of the Ottoman Empire and matches a crucial time in the life of the prototype beast—1924 in Adolf Hitler's life. It is also a pivotal time for the man that wants to bring back the Ottoman Empire. President Erdogan of Turkey views March 3rd, 2024 as the target date for reinstating the new Ottoman Empire—just as our biblical pattern predicted that the Ottoman Empire must be reestablished sometime in the future. Since a leader from the nation of Turkey ended the old Ottoman Empire, a leader from the nation of Turkey must be the one to revive the new Ottoman Empire.

We need to emphasize something again. No one knows when these things are going to come to pass because the Lord is the one who is ultimately in control of things. We are not setting

---

[22] Walid Shoebat, Erdogan of Turkey Literally Resurrects the Image of the Ottoman Beast and Vows that all Who Defy Him Will be Beheaded, http://shoebat.com/2017/07/18/erdogan-of-turkey-literally-resurrects-the-image-of-the-beast-and-vows-that-all-who-defy-him-will-be-beheaded.

dates or predicting the future because only God knows these things. However, it is important to be aware of times that can be of critical importance in our lives and in the lives of our loved ones. Being ignorant of these things does not lend any understanding of how things may come to pass in the future. We need to search for all the answers we can so we will be a resource to those who don't understand what is happening and need the insight of biblical patterns.

Hitler's Curious Influence in Turkey

There is a rather bizarre way that Adolf Hitler is still having an impact in the nation of Turkey. His book, *Mein Kampf*, has become a national best seller in Turkey. Israel National News reported that sales of *Mein Kampf* exceeded 50,000 copies in March of 2005.[23] Other Islamic countries have followed the example of Turkey and have embraced Hitler's book also, making it one of the most sought after books in all of Islam. Syria's ruling Baath party officials expressed their admiration for the ideals of anti-Semitism and Nazism expressed in the pages of Hitler's book.[24]

Long after Hitler's death, he is still having an influence as a prototype beast leader in the nation that will soon bring back the Ottoman Empire, the nation of Turkey. President Erdogan embraces many of the ideas of Hitler. In many ways they had the same struggles

Erdogan's life has mirrored Hitler's life in many different ways. For example:

---

23 Contact Editor, Hitler's *Mein Kampf* a Best-Seller in Turkey, Israel National News, http://www.israelnationalnews.com/News/News.aspx/78801
24 Ibid

- President Erdogan has a speaking style that is reminiscent of Hitler's style. He begins his speeches softly and then raises the intensity to a fever pitch. Many reporters have observed that Erdogan sounds like Hitler when he speaks.
- Both men display fierce nationalism.
- Hitler and Erdogan both displayed hatred for the Jews.
- Both Hitler and Erdogan spent time in jail—Hitler for the Beer Hall Putsch and Erdogan was in jail for incitement to violence in Turkey from March 24th, 1999 to July 27th, 1999.[25]
- Both men were targeted by their political enemies.
- Both men silenced and swept aside their political enemies.
- Hitler and Erdogan united the military behind them. Erdogan accomplished this after the coup attempt in July of 2016. He purged the military of all that opposed him and jailed all of the high ranking military forces that were a part of the coup attempt.
- Both men had visions of an empire to rule the world. Hitler had Germany to help him achieve his goals, and President Erdogan has the entire Muslim world to help him achieve his Hegemony if he can unite them.

---

25 Wikipedia, Recep Tayyip Erdogan, Imprisonment, https://en.wikipedia.org/wiki/Recep_Tayyip_Erdo%C4%9Fan

The Prototype Pattern for Revealing the Eighth Beast Empire

- There is a striking similarity in the physical appearance of both men. Here is a picture of Adolf Hitler and President Erdogan side by side. The physical resemblance is uncanny.

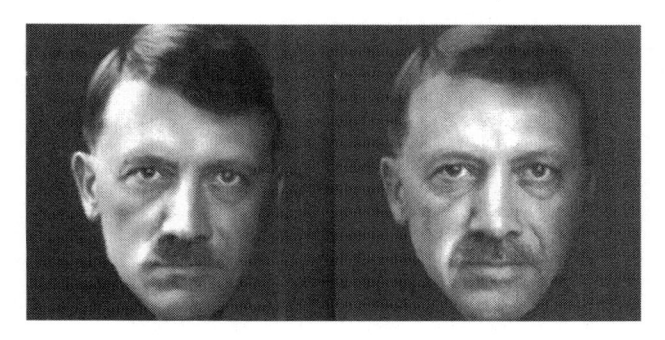

Can President Erdogan of Turkey achieve his dream of a renewed Ottoman Empire? Will the new Ottoman Empire become the eighth beast empire portrayed in end time prophecies? The biblical pattern we have been studying points to a strong leader emerging in Turkey and reviving the Ottoman Empire. If it isn't President Erdogan then another strong leader in Turkey must rise to take his place. The problem is, the Muslim world is not ready to stand and embrace President Erdogan of Turkey as their leader. There are substantial obstacles that stand in his way. The Islamic world has erected barriers to prevent this from happening. What is absolutely amazing is the fact that the Bible describes another intersecting pattern that stands in the way of the complete fulfillment of the beast kingdom pattern—a barrier that must come down before President Erdogan can achieve his goals. That intersecting pattern is shrouded in mystery and is an enigmatic event that almost no one in the western world has seen coming. Until this event happens, President Erdogan of Turkey will have a hard time realizing his dreams. An enigma shrouded in a mystery is waiting to happen, and all things are pointing to the near fulfillment of this barrier coming down. When the intersecting pattern barrier is fulfilled, nothing will be left standing in the way of Recep Tayyip Erdogan and the rise of the new Ottoman Empire.

CHAPTER NINE

The Barrier to the Rise of the Eighth Beast Empire

If we were to ask what one of the greatest mysteries of the Bible was, what would be the response? There are many different possibilities that come to mind. What if we were to narrow down our inquiry even further and say that this great mystery has to be called a mystery in the Bible? And what if the word mystery was intertwined with the title of this enigmatic thing? Wouldn't it be imperative that we correctly identify the entity the Bible was talking about?

Not only is it imperative that we get this identity correct, but it is crucial for the correct understanding of what the Bible is trying to tell us.

Let's introduce that mysterious entity now. It is called "Mystery Babylon" in the Bible. What is Mystery Babylon and where can we find more about it in God's Word?

Mystery Babylon

We are never told exactly what Mystery Babylon is in the Bible. However, we are given many clues that will help us with the identification of this enigmatic entity. What is truly astounding is the fact that this entity connects with the important beast empires we have been studying. Let's take a look at that connection. We find the reference to Mystery Babylon in Revelation where John is shown the following:

> So he carried me away in the spirit into the wilderness: and I saw a woman sit upon a scarlet colored beast, full of names of blasphemy, having seven heads and ten horns. And the woman was arrayed in purple and scarlet color, and decked with gold and precious stones and pearls, having a golden cup in her hand full of abominations and filthiness of her fornication: And upon her forehead was a name written, Mystery, Babylon the Great, The Mother of Harlots and Abominations of the Earth. (Revelation 17:3-5)

There is a lot to discover in this passage. To make our task a little bit simpler, let's use what we have learned up to this point and see if this can help open the door to understanding this rather complex passage. This verse alludes to something that has seven heads and ten horns. From what we have already discovered in the beastly kingdom prophecies, the seven heads represent seven different dynasties of the Islamic Caliphate, and the ten horns were ten different leaders in those Islamic dynasties. From this fact alone we can surmise that this passage is referring to the Islamic world and whatever Mystery Babylon is will somehow pertain to the Islamic world.

The Barrier to the Rise of the Eighth Beast Empire

Before we try to interpret this passage we need to know more about Mystery Babylon. Is Mystery Babylon a concept, an idea, a place or a person? The imagery of Mystery Babylon is connected and linked with a woman because the Mystery Babylon title is found written on the woman's forehead. (Revelation 17:5) The woman and Mystery Babylon are so intrinsically linked that the title defines the woman. They are connected to the point that they are inseparably linked. The woman is depicted in the following ways:

- She is depicted as a great whore that sits upon many waters. (Revelation 17:1)
- The woman sits upon a scarlet colored beast that has seven heads and ten horns. (Revelation 17: 3) Since we know that the seven headed beast represents the seven different Islamic Caliphate dynasties and ten leaders, then this means that the woman seen riding the beast is somehow in a controlling position over the Islamic Caliphates and leaders. Somehow the woman controls the beast empires and the leaders of those beast empires.

So who is the woman described in these passages? And what power can control all of Islam and the Islamic dynasties?

We are given the critical clue later on in Revelation. It says that the woman is a great city:

And the woman which thou sawest is that great city, which reigneth over the kings of the earth.
(Revelation 17:18)

So now we know that the woman depicted in these passages is a great city—not an idea or a concept, but an actual city. And the great city rules over the Islamic dynasties and kings. From this description alone we can rule out many of the great cities of the world because they don't rule over the Islamic world. The city can't be New York, or Rome, or Jerusalem or even Washington DC. It must be a great city that Islam controls. Rather than guessing what Islamic city is being talked about in these passages, we need more clues to narrow down our search. If we look more closely at the description given us by the Apostle John, then the list of candidate cities is narrowed down to just one.

There is an excellent book that goes through all of the clues to the identity of Mystery Babylon very thoroughly and I would highly recommend that you read it. It is called *"Mystery Babylon, Unlocking the Bible's Greatest Prophetic Mystery,"* and it was written by Joel Richardson. When you read this book it leaves little doubt about which city in the Islamic World is being referenced in Revelation. Here are some of the key identifiers that will unlock the identity of this city.

- When John experienced the vision of Mystery Babylon he was shown a city in the wilderness. (Revelation 17:3) What is a wilderness in Middle Eastern context? The Greek word used for wilderness is "eremos," and in Greek eremos denotes a lonely, deserted, solitary place signifying a desert. This word is used in two other places in the Bible—the Israelites wandered in the wilderness (eremos) for 40 years. Where were they wandering? They were in the Sinai,

Negev and Jordanian deserts. Jesus went into the wilderness (eremos) to be tempted. (Matthew 4:1) Where was He during that time? He was in the desert. This means that Mystery Babylon is a desert city. We must thank Joel Richardson and his book for the insight on this crucial point.

- Mystery Babylon is a place where an abomination to God is located. Anything that is worshipped instead of God is an abomination to God.

- This abomination to God is covered with names full of blasphemy. (Revelation 17:3)

- Mystery Babylon controls the entire Islamic world because all of the Muslim world must come to the place that Mystery Babylon is located at least once in their lifetime. In this way Mystery Babylon controls Islamic Dynasties and Kings.

- The woman of Mystery Babylon is drunken with the blood of the saints and with the blood of the martyrs of Jesus. (Revelation 17:6) The most violent and blood thirsty form of radical Islam is known as Wahhabism and is found in the country harboring Mystery Babylon. The Wahhabist form of Islam has spawned Al Qaeda, the Taliban, Boko Haram and ISIS and these groups are responsible for hundreds of thousands of deaths. The Wahhabist brand of Islam believes that if you are not following the old ways of Islam practiced by the ancestors and embrace anything modern or influenced by the western world then you are worthy of death.

- The woman (city) sits on seven hills. (Revelation 17:9) There is a city in the Islamic world in a desert that sits on seven hills. This final clue allows us to positively identify the city in question. Here are the seven hills that this infamous city sits on:
  1. Jabal abu Siba'
  2. Jabal Safa
  3. Jabal Marwah
  4. Jabal abu Milhah
  5. Jabal abu Ma'aya
  6. Jabal abu Hulayah
  7. Jabal abu Ghuzlan

There can be no doubt as to the identity of the city in question. The city is **Mecca** in Saudi Arabia. **Mecca fits the description of the woman in Revelation in every aspect that is described**. The city of Mecca has been intrinsically connected with the Islamic religion from the time of Muhammad. It was the chief city in Muhammad's life, and continues to this day to be the chief city in the Muslim world. Every faithful Muslim must come to this city at least once in their life during the Hajj, a religious pilgrimage to the foremost place in Mecca.

What is it about Mecca that has such a hold on the Islamic world? Why does all of Islam insist on coming to Mecca? What are they doing in Mecca that holds such control over all Muslims?

The answer to that question is the essence of Mystery Babylon itself. Mystery Babylon was found inscribed on the forehead of the woman. It is the place from which every thought in the

Muslim world is centered. It is the chief idea and the very core of Islam. Which place in the city of Mecca are we talking about?

Let's use the clues given to us in the Bible to further pinpoint this exact location in Mecca. Is there any place in Mecca that is adorned with purple and scarlet and is bejeweled with precious stones and pearls? (Revelation 17:4) Is there any place in the city where phrases that are considered blasphemous to the Lord are written? (Revelation 17:3) Is there any place in Mecca that is the center of a false religion? (Revelation 17:5) Is there a place in Mecca that is decked out in gold? (Revelation 17:4) Is there any place in Mecca that God would consider the mother of harlots and abominations of the earth? (Revelation 17:5)

If there is—then this is the place where Mystery Babylon is located. It is the very head and center of thought of Mystery Babylon. Let me show you just such a place in Mecca:

This is the Kaaba and it sits in the Sacred Mosque in Mecca. This is the place where every devout Muslim must come at least once in their life. This is the center of the Islamic religion. This is the place that every Muslim faces toward during their prayers throughout the day. This is the place where something other than God is worship with a fever and intensity that almost defies description. At the very center of their adoration is a 60 by 60 foot cube called the Kaaba.

Let's take a closer look at the Kaaba. There are some things we need to know about this mysterious object.

This is a close up view of the Kaaba. One thing very noticeable is the gold and silver stitching on the cloth that covers this structure. To most of us the stitching looks like simple decorations and benign sayings that embellish the covering.

Upon closer examination however, we find that the stitching contains phrases blaspheming God and stating how Allah is greater than God. These gold and silver embroiderments also represent different Islamic dynasties and various leaders in Islam. The doors of the Kaaba are made out of pure gold weighing hundreds of pounds. Inside the doors of the Kaaba are purple and scarlet coverings lining the walls. Precious stones and pearls adorn the interior of this structure and in the very center of the Kaaba is a black meteorite stone.

For Christians, Jesus Christ is our rock and the person in whom we place our trust. In Islam, a black meteorite stone fallen from the sky is the object of their veneration. This reminds us of a phrase found in Revelation where it says that a "star fell from heaven unto the earth." (Revelation 9:1) The black meteorite stone is the representation of that fallen star. One day in the future a star will fall from heaven and it will be a representation of Satan, the devil. Its fall from heaven will unleash havoc and destruction upon the earth that the world has never seen. And here in the center of the Kaaba is a prototype of that fallen star. This is the place of Mystery Babylon.

The Identity of the Woman Riding the Beast

Who is it that controls Mecca and access to the Kaaba? The country that controls Mecca controls the entire Islamic world. The country that controls Mecca is the woman riding the beast and the country controlling the seven heads of the Caliphate dynasty. What county is that?

It is the nation of Saudi Arabia and the house of Saud. Saudi Arabia is the woman riding the beast. And Saudi Arabia is not about to give up control of the city of Mecca. They derive too much income from visitors to the Kaaba to ever relinquish control. This places Saudi Arabia in a dominating position over all of Islam, and makes Saudi Arabia the controlling force in the Islamic world. Combined with the power of their considerable oil wealth, Saudi Arabia is a force to be reckoned with.

The Turkish View of Saudi Arabia

To the leader trying to bring back the Ottoman Empire, Saudi Arabia is a substantial obstacle. President Erdogan of Turkey knows that Saudi Arabia is seen as the most influential leader in the Islamic world, and the Saudis are virtually immune to economic pressure due to their considerable oil revenues. Saudi Arabia is a barrier that must be overcome for Turkey to take its proper place and bring back the Ottoman Empire.

An old wound has been festering with those in Turkey since Lawrence of Arabia united the Saudis with the Hashemite's of Iraq and Syria in WW1 to crush the old Ottoman Empire. The nation of Turkey and its leader President Erdogan has not forgotten the Saudis belligerent and traitorous attacks against them. Turkey is waiting for the right opportunity to strike back at those who destroyed the old Ottoman Empire.

Unbeknownst to them, the Bible has already recorded this coming conflict in its pages thousands of years ago. A battle is brewing in the Islamic world, and the Bible has already detailed the outcome of this coming cataclysmic struggle in biblical patterns waiting for us to examine. Understanding these biblical patterns will be the key to unlocking end time events. The time for revealing the fate of the woman (Mecca in Saudi Arabia) in this biblical pattern is now.

CHAPTER TEN

The Dilemma of Saudi Arabia

There is a place in God's Word that details the destruction of the woman (Mecca in Saudi Arabia) controlling the beast. Before we get into that, we need to ask a question. How did the city of Mecca, controlled by the government of Saudi Arabia, get to the point where it is going to be destroyed? What makes a city and a government so bad that it is better off destroyed?

While there may be many answers to this question, here is a list of some of the most egregious offenses perpetrated or influenced by Mecca and Saudi Arabia.

Wahhabism

We have touched on the fact that Saudi Arabia is the home of the Wahhabist branch of Islam. What is Wahhabism and what are the implications of Wahhabist thought?

Wahhabism is a belief system in the Muslim faith that arose from the teachings of Muhammad ibn Abdul Wahhab, a Sunni cleric born in 1703. He taught that Islam had strayed from their pure faith by being corrupted by superstition and the influences of Christians and Jews. He founded the "Salafist" branch of Islam that taught that the Muslim religion needed to get back to the pure form of Islam practiced by the early ancestors and followers of the prophet Muhammad. In fact, the word "Salaf" means "ancestor" in Arabic.

Wahhabist thoughts have become the basis for many of the most radical Islamists, including Al-Qaeda in the Middle East, the Taliban in Afghanistan, Boko Haram in Africa, and most recently ISIS in Syria and Iraq. There is no question that these groups have killed thousands of people that do not agree with them. One of the most recent atrocities has been perpetrated by ISIS under the direction of the Caliphate led by Abu Bakr al-Baghdadi. The Caliphate targeted Christian communities living in the Sinjar and Nineveh Plain regions and almost succeeded in exterminating the entire Christian population in these areas. One of the surviving leaders of the Yezidi Christians made it to America and testified before Congress. Mizra Ismail, the chairman of the Yezidi Human Rights Organization-International, testified before Congress on December 9, 2015, and related the following account:

> Because we are not Muslims and because our path is the path of peace...we are being burned alive. There are thousands of young Yezidi women, girls, and even children, who as I speak, have been enslaved and forced into sexual slavery. These girls are subjected to daily, multiple rapes by ISIS monsters. According to many escaped women and girls whom I talked to in Northern Iraq, the abducted Yezidis, mostly women and children, number over 7,000. Some of those women and girls have

had to watch 7, 8, and 9 year old children bleed to death before their eyes, after being raped by ISIS militia multiple times a day...I met mothers, whose children were torn from them by ISIS. These same mothers came to plead for the return of their children, only to be informed, that they, the mothers, had been fed the flesh of their own children by ISIS. Children murdered, then fed to their own mothers...ISIS militia have burned many Yezidi girls alive for refusing to convert and marry ISIS men. Young Yezidi boys are being trained to be jihadist and suicide bombers. All of our temples in the ISIS controlled area are exploded and destroyed...What I have just recounted to you, what has happened to the Yezidis and Chaldo-Assyrian Christians and other minorities in Sinjar and in the Nineveh Plain is nothing less than genocide, according to the UN definition.[26]

These were the actions of the Wahhabist-inspired Caliphate of Abu Bakr al-Baghdadi and the troops loyal to him. After this testimony was heard, the leaders of the world begrudgingly acknowledged these horrific acts of terror, and then dismissed them as if these actions were some sort of aberration and not the belief system of Muslims who were loyal to the Caliphate. The Wahhabist brand of Islam spawned by Saudi Arabia and the actions of the followers of the new Caliphate are almost too horrendous to even contemplate. Millions of Islamic people following the directives of the new Caliphate do recognize the horrendous acts described above as being characteristic of Islam, and they have the fingerprints and unspoken approval

---

26 Zachary Leshin, "Yezidi Leader Tells Congress: 'Because We Are Not Muslims...We Are Being Burned Alive,'" cnsnews.com, December 11, 2015, http://www.cnsnews.com/news/article/zachary-leshin/congressional-testimony-because-we-are-not-muslims-we-are-being-burned-alive.

of Saudi Arabia stamped all over them. These are the actions that the woman and Mystery Babylon are unleashing in the world. What other things has Mystery Babylon unleashed?

Drunk on the Blood of the Saints and the Martyrs of Jesus

The destruction of the Yezidi Christians is just the latest in a series of atrocities carried out by those loyal to Mystery Babylon. Before the Yezidis, over a million Armenians were killed by directions coming from the Islamic Caliphate and the whispered directives coming from Mystery Babylon. Before the Armenians, countless others were killed by warriors of the mystery religion inspired by Mecca. The vast majority of those battles took place around the Mediterranean Sea. If you plot out the location of the battles fought by Islamic forces loyal to the Caliphate through the ages, you will find that hundreds of battles were fought against Christianity and the Church around the Mediterranean Sea. Thousands and thousands of Christians have died throughout the ages fighting battles against Islamic warriors in Spain, Corsica, Sicily, Italy, the Balkan regions, Greece, Turkey, the Middle East and Northern Africa. The "Sea" the beast arises from in Revelation 13 is synonymous with the Mediterranean Sea and so many Christians have been killed by warriors of the Mystery religion that it is almost impossible to number them.

This is exactly the way the woman is portrayed in God's Word. John says:

> And I saw the woman drunken with the blood of the saints, and with the blood of the martyrs of Jesus... (Revelation 17:6)

The warriors of Mecca have targeted the church and nations around the Mediterranean Sea and the beast has destroyed many of them. This too was predicted in God's Word.

> And it was given unto him to make war with the saints, and to overcome them: and power was given him over all kindreds, and tongues, and nations. (Revelation 13:7)

The followers of Mystery Babylon have been so successful that they can be characterized as being literally "drunken with the blood of the saints." This is another contributing factor that has marked Mecca as being worthy of destruction.

Mother of Harlots and Abominations

The nation of Saudi Arabia has been linked with other atrocities including slavery and forced sexual slavery and prostitution. While this may seem shocking to most of the world where involuntary servitude and forced sexual acts have been outlawed, it is openly acknowledged by leading clerics in Saudi Arabia. The author of Saudi Arabia's religious curriculum and one of the nation's leading authorities on Islam, Sheik Saleh Al-Fawzan has stated that "Slavery is a part of Islam," according to the Saudi Information Agency. He is also quoted as saying that "Slavery is part of jihad, and jihad will remain as long as there is Islam."[27] If this Sheik was speaking for himself then maybe we could ignore his words, but this man's religious books are the curriculum for over five million Saudi students. Slavery is so ingrained in the Saudi culture that many Saudi nationals have accepted slavery as normal. Many

---

27   Saudi Sheik: "Slavery is a part of Islam," WorldNetDaily, November 10, 2003, www.wnd.com/news/article.asp?Article ID=35518 (Accessed 21 December 2010)

women who have come to the country for working opportunities, including women from Bangladesh, India, Sri Lanka, Nepal, Pakistan, the Philippines, Indonesia, Sudan, Ethiopia and other countries from the Far East, have suffered from conditions of slavery, physical and sexual abuse, withholding of passports, commercial prostitution, and human trafficking.[28] So many women have been forced into prostitution and involuntary sexual slavery that Saudi Arabia is aptly described as the "Mother of Harlots."

The slavery is not limited to women and men but also includes children. The Pakistan Press International reported that children were freed from slavery in Saudi Arabia and other Arabic nations and returned to their home countries for rehabilitation from slavery and other horrendous abuse situations.[29]

There are approximately 6.4 million foreign workers in Saudi Arabia at this time and there are hundreds of articles describing abominable situations for many of these workers. While the nation of Saudi Arabia may like to project an image of benign benevolence to others, the real story of those that have suffered at their hands is another story.

Lest we forget, fifteen of the nineteen hijackers on 9/11 were citizens of Saudi Arabia. The loss of life and the damage that those hijackers inflicted on America will never be forgotten.

These are just a few examples of why Saudi Arabia and the Mystery Babylon city of Mecca face judgment and impending

---

28 Human Trafficking and Modern-day Slavery, Kingdom of Saudi Arabia, http://gvnet.com/humantrafficking/Saudi Arabia.htm
29 Trafficking and forced labour of children in the United Arab Emirates continues, Pakistan Press International PPI, Lahore, 09 October 2004, (accessed 11 September 2011.)

destruction. One could also list the fact that Mecca is the center of global idolatry to its list of offenses. Anything worshipped other than God is a form of idolatry and the meteorite stone enclosed in the Kaaba certainly qualifies as such. More people come to Mecca to worship this symbol of Mystery Babylon that any other place in the world. Mecca has become the number one tourist destination in the world because of all the Muslims embarking on the Hajj pilgrimage that is required at least once in their lives. During the season of the Hajj, so many Muslims are in Mecca and the surrounding areas that massive tent cities must be set up to house all of the visitors. This makes Mecca the most visited city in the world.

Does God Give Warnings to Nations?

When a nation has influenced and been the perpetrator of as many crimes as Saudi Arabia, and houses and openly encourages the worship of a structure that their religious leaders have used as inspiration to carry out horrendous and murderous missions in the world, does God give a warning to that nation of its impending judgment?

Yes He does.

The question then becomes, has Saudi Arabia been given a warning of their impending destruction and have they been granted time to change their ways?

The astounding answer to this question is that yes, Saudi Arabia has been given a warning and the warning was given in such a way that all that witnessed it have stated that it was **an act of God**. In fact, the place this warning was given was in **the heart of Mystery Babylon on the very structure that**

houses the Kaaba. And what is most astonishing of all is the fact that this warning was given **on the same day in history** emissaries of Saudi Arabia perpetrated one of their most infamous acts of terrorism in the United States.

A camera near the Sacred Mosque in Mecca captured an image of this warning. The Sacred Mosque in Mecca is the structure that houses the Kaaba and is considered the most renowned mosque in all of Islam. On 9/11 in 2015, the following image was caught on camera:

A lightning bolt struck a crane working on the Sacred Mosque in Mecca, Saudi Arabia. The crane was damaged, but this was just a prelude to something that would happen latter in the day. On the same day, 9/11 in 2015, at around 5 PM, a fierce wind storm began to form. Those who witnessed this storm said that it was not a normal wind storm. It formed within a matter of minutes, the skies darkened and soon the Sacred Mosque was enveloped by hurricane force winds. The winds increased in intensity until the sounds of rending and grinding metal could be heard amidst the sounds of the destructive winds. A huge crane wrenched free of its restraints and crashed through a portion of the Sacred Mosque, causing significant damage to the structure.

The storm quickly dissipated soon after, leaving those that witnessed this incident astonished by the sequence of events that unfolded on that day. The witnesses were all united on one startling impression about the lighting strike and the sudden storm—it was an act of God that had overwhelmed Mecca on 9/11 in 2015.

What was most unusual about the crane that was struck by lightning and collapsed that day was that this particular crane was owned by the Bin Laden construction group. There were over 100 cranes operating in Mecca that day, and this particular crane was one of the few owned by the Bin Laden construction conglomerate, by the father of Osama Bin Laden.[30] Osama Bin Laden was the man most responsible for coordinating the attacks that devastated the United States on 9/11 in 2001. Most of the people he recruited for the terrorist attacks in the United States were citizens of Saudi Arabia. It is absolutely astonishing that a crane owned by the Bin Laden family would crash through the most renowned Mosque in Islam on the anniversary of 9/11. This crane crash was rated the deadliest crane crash to ever happen in the world with 107 people dying immediately and another four people dying later as a result of their injuries.

A Reverse 9/11

This was just the first in a series of events that served as a warning to the nation of Saudi Arabia that God would hold them accountable for their actions. This was not the end of catastrophes for Saudi Arabia that would strike in September of that year. Thirteen days later on September 24th, 2015, the most tragic event ever to happen in the history of the Hajj pilgrimage took place. What was unusual for this tragedy was that it impacted those traveling to the heart of Mystery Babylon; those going to the Sacred Mosque to worship the Kaaba. On September 24th, large crowds of people began walking toward the Kaaba when suddenly the crowds began surging forward until they were stopped by the huge walls along the way. The

---

30 Gina Cassini, "Breaking: You Won't Believe Who Owned The Crane That Collapsed In Mecca On 9/11 Anniversary," Top Right News, 12 September 2015, http://toprightnews.com/breaking-you-won't-believe-who-owned-the-crane-that-collapsed-in-mecca-today/.

crush of the crowds degenerated into a stampede until people began to be crushed from the weight of the surging masses. Before order was restored, 2411 people were crushed to death by the out of control crowds. This is the number of deaths according to Al Jazeera America and the associated press.[31]

As the dust settled from both of these tragedies, something else happened that placed Saudi Arabia on the brink of financial disaster. It was something that experts around the world said could never happen in modern times. The price of oil collapsed. It didn't just fall a little, it plunged to the point where most countries could not cover the price of oil production. The price of oil collapsed so dramatically that Saudi Arabia, the country known the world over as the king of oil producers, was left scrambling for a way to keep its economy from imploding. Faced with this precarious position, Saudi Arabia had to borrow money for the first time in their history just to keep their economy functioning.

The Warning to Saudi Arabia

Saudi Arabia had been given a warning from God that they need to change their ways. The warning was given in such a way that it mimicked a reverse 9/11 pattern in their own country. Let's consider the facts about the reverse 9/11 pattern that struck Saudi Arabia in September of 2015.

- A lightning bolt stuck a crane connected to the Sacred Mosque on 9/11, 2015. Lightning strikes have been signified as an "Act of God" by almost

---

[31] The Associated Press, "Over 2,400 killed in September Saudi Hajj Stampede," Al Jazeera America, 10 December 2015, http://america.aljezeera.com/articles/2015/12/10/over-2400-killed-in-saudi-hajj-stampede.html.

every culture in the world. The fact that lightning struck this particular crane would become significant later that day.

- A severe weather phenomenon developed quickly within a matter of moments later in the afternoon of 9/11 and became a ferocious wind storm. The anomalous storm toppled the crane struck by lightning into the Sacred Mosque, in the heart of Mecca, Mystery Babylon. People witnessing the event called it an "Act of God." The storm dissipated rapidly after the crane toppled into the Sacred Mosque.

- The crane that collapsed was owned by the Bin Laden family, specifically by the father of Osama Bin Laden and the Bin Laden construction conglomerate. As a result of this incident, the Bin Laden construction group was cited and held responsible for the accident. Their construction contracts were suspended until they could demonstrate compliance to all safety codes enforced by Saudi Arabia. Osama Bin Laden's father pleaded that he could not be held responsible for an "Act of God" and pleaded for leniency at the hands of the Saudi court system. The outcomes of these proceedings were never made public.

- On September 24th, 2015, a crowd on the outskirts of Mecca began their walk toward the Kaaba contained within the Sacred Mosque. No one knows how it began exactly, but the mass of people began surging forward until there was a literal stampeded of people pushing forward and crushing others against the walls lining the path. At least 2411 people were killed in the crush of the crowds according to Al Jazeera. This became the deadliest disaster to ever happen in the history of the Hajj pilgrimage.

- The price of oil collapsed on world markets in the fall of 2015 sending the economy of Saudi Arabia into a downward spiral. The repercussions of this event are still having an economic impact on the Saudis to this day.

- The facts that these events started on the anniversary of 9/11, fourteen years after the original 9/11 in the United States, and happened in the country where the majority of the 9/11 hijackers came from is astonishing. Saudi Arabia suffered their own reverse 9/11 event in 2015, but it did not come from throngs of angry Americans. It came as a warning from God.

God Holds Nations Accountable

There are many in the world today that feel they can do as they wish and that they will not be held accountable for whatever they do. That is not the case. God holds both people and nations accountable for their actions.

There is a fundamental truth that should be observed by the adherents of any religion. You do not have the right in the name of any religion to go out and kill others, or force others to convert to your religion unwillingly. If you religion gains

converts by the force of the sword, then by the force of the sword that religion will be destroyed.

The nation of Saudi Arabia stands on the edge of a precipice. It is the home of Mystery Babylon and has been given a warning by God. What happens next is up to Saudi Arabia. How much time have they been given to change their ways in this warning? No one knows the answer to that question but God Himself.

In a biblical pattern, contained in God's Word, is an account of a coming war in Islam. The players in this future conflict are in place, the stage has been set, and now all that needs to happen is for a fuse to be lit to ignite this war. It's now time to examine "The Coming War in Islam."

One thing is for certain, Saudi Arabia will be the epicenter of this future war.

CHAPTER ELEVEN

The Coming Showdown in Islam

What is the basis for saying that there is going to be a war amongst Islamic countries? It comes from God's Word and is written in the Book of Revelation. Let's take a look at that passage.

> The beast and the ten horns you saw will hate the prostitute. They will bring her to ruin and leave her naked; they will eat her flesh and burn her with fire. For God has put it into their hearts to accomplish his purpose by agreeing to hand over to the beast their royal authority until God's words are fulfilled. The woman you saw is the great city that rules over the kings of the earth. (Revelation 17:16-18 NIV)

We need to review some identities so we know what this passage is talking about. The beast as we have discovered before is the Islamic religion led by the Caliphate. The ten horns are leaders or kings from ten Islamic countries that have not been placed in positions of power as yet (Revelation 17:12) but will be placed in a position of power by the leader of the eighth beastly kingdom (the renewed Ottoman Empire.) The prostitute is the city of Mecca which is led and controlled by the nation of Saudi Arabia.

Based on what we have learned by our insight from the biblical patterns we have studied, we can make some conclusions about what this passage is saying. Turkey, the headquarters of the soon to be new Ottoman Empire and Islamic Caliphate, and an alliance of leaders from ten Islamic countries, are going to be so incensed with Saudi Arabia, the country controlling the city of Mecca, that they are going to make war with Saudi Arabia and leave the nation and the city of Mecca desolate and in ruins. **Turkey and its allies are going to attack Saudi Arabia.**

This is the war that will soon happen in Islam. This is the war that will change everything and remove the barrier from Turkey taking over the entire Muslim world and the Islamic Caliphate and making Turkey the headquarters of the renewed Ottoman Empire and the eighth beastly kingdom in biblical prophecy.

What do we know about this war?

We can gather many insights about this future war by reviewing what we are told in God's Word. One of the first clues we are given is that the city of Mecca is going to be burnt with fire. We are told that in the following passages:

- "and shall…burn her with fire." (Revelation 17:16)
- "and she shall be utterly burned with fire…" (Revelation 18:8)
- "they shall see the smoke of her burning." (Revelation 18:9)

- "and cried when they saw the smoke of her burning." (Revelation 18:18)

One of the most surprising things is the suddenness in which the burning shall occur. The desolation shall happen within one hour.

- Alas, alas, that great city Babylon, that mighty city! For in one hour is thy judgment come. (Revelation 18:10)
- For in one hour so great riches is come to nought. (Revelation 18:17)
- For in one hour is she made desolate. (Revelation 18:19)

However it is going to happen, the destruction of Mystery Babylon, Mecca, is going to take place within one hour. When the destruction is complete, the city of Mecca is never going to be inhabited again.

> With such violence the great city of Babylon will be thrown down, never to be found again. The music of harpists and musicians, pipers and trumpeters, will never be heard in you again. No worker of any trade will ever be found in you again. The sound of a millstone will never be heard in you again. The light of a lamp will never shine in you again. The voice of bridegroom and bride will never be heard in you again. (Revelation 18:21-23 NIV)

When the destruction of Mecca occurs, it will be witnessed by several groups of people. One of these groups is captains of ships and sailors. Mecca is close enough to the Red Sea that the smoke of its burning will be witnessed by those making a living by commerce on the sea. Saudi Arabia's primary export is oil, and there are hundreds of sea captains hauling oil all over the world. They will be devastated when Mecca is destroyed.

> Every sea captain, and all who travel by ship, the sailors, and all who earn their living from the sea, will stand far off. When they see the smoke of her burning, they will exclaim, was there ever a city like this great city? They will throw dust on their heads, and with weeping and mourning cry out: Woe! Woe to you, great city, where all who had ships on the sea became rich through her wealth! In one hour she has been brought to ruin! (Revelation 18:17-19 NIV)

The sea captains will not be the only ones mourning the destruction of Mecca. The merchants of the earth and merchant ships will be distraught also. Saudi Arabia is one of the biggest consumer nations in the entire world because they produce very little in their own country. All of the goods they need have to be transported into Saudi Arabia. When the merchants of the earth witness the destruction of Mecca they will be devastated by the realization that they will no longer be able to sell their products in the lucrative market of Mecca. Trade to all of Saudi Arabia will be disrupted.

> The merchants of the earth will weep and mourn over her because no one buys their cargoes anymore—cargoes of gold, silver, precious stones and pearls; fine linen, purple, silk and scarlet cloth; every sort of citron wood, and articles of every kind made of ivory, costly wood,

bronze, iron and marble; cargoes of cinnamon and spice, of incense, myrrh and frankincense, of wine and olive oil, of fine flour and wheat; cattle and sheep; horses and carriages; and human beings sold as slaves. They will say, "The fruit you longed for is gone from you. All your luxury and splendor have vanished, never to be recovered." The merchants who sold these things and gained their wealth from her will stand far off, terrified at her torment. They will weep and mourn and cry out: Woe! Woe to you, great city, dressed in fine linen, purple and scarlet, and glittering with gold, precious stones and pearls! In one hour such great wealth has been brought to ruin! (Revelation 18:11-17 NIV)

You may wonder how this destruction is going to be accomplished. While ultimately the ruin of Mecca is going to come as a judgment from God, it is going to be carried out by the nation of Turkey as the leader of the eighth beast empire, and a coalition of leaders from ten different Islamic countries. How do we know this? We are told that God would use the beast and the ten leaders to accomplish this feat in His Word where it says that "God has put it in their hearts to accomplish his purpose." (Revelation 17:17)

The war is going to be over very rapidly. When Turkey and the coalition of ten other Islamic countries decide to strike, Mecca is going to be obliterated within one hour and Saudi Arabia will be overthrown as the leading power in the Islamic world. Saudi Arabia will then become a vassal state to Turkey and will be controlled by the Islamic Caliphate based in Turkey.

None of this has happened as of this time. Yet God's Word is very clear when we use the insight we have gained from our knowledge of the biblical pattern that this war in Islam is going to happen in the future. When the time is right according to God's purposes, this war will take place.

Why do other Muslim countries hate Saudi Arabia?

Why do Turkey and other Muslim nations hold such great animosity with regard to Saudi Arabia? There are several reasons this is the case, but the following are some of the greatest reasons:

- Saudi Arabia united with the Hashemite kings of Iraq and Syria under the leadership of Lawrence of Arabia to defeat the final vestiges of the Ottoman Empire in WW1. The Ottoman Empire was headquartered in Turkey and Turkey has never forgotten this betrayal by their Muslim brothers of one of the greatest dynasties in the Islamic world. With the formation of the new Ottoman Empire, Saudi Arabia will be held accountable for their part in the overthrow of the old Ottoman Empire. Saudi Arabia must be destroyed to legitimize the new Ottoman Empire.

- Saudi Arabia preaches the Wahhabist form of Islam and pretends to be pious, and yet some of the most outrageous breaches of the Muslim conduct can be found within the nation of Saudi Arabia. The royal house of Saud is an example of some of the most reckless forms of hedonism found in the world today. There are stories of rampant drug abuse, serial rape, orgies, forced homosexuality, child molestation and other forms of perversity and utter corruption in the ruling family in control of Saudi Arabia.[32] The irony is that Saudi Arabia thinks that they are the example for what a nation in the Islamic world should look like. Many Muslim nations cannot tolerate the hypocrisy coming from the supposed model nation of Islam and think that Saudi Arabia should be removed from power.

- Saudi Arabia controls the Muslim world because the most sacred shrine in all of Islam sits in Mecca. The Masjid al-Haram, or Sacred Mosque, houses the Kaaba, and all faithful Muslims are expected to make a pilgrimage to the Sacred Mosque at least once in their lifetimes. This gives Saudi Arabia a tremendous amount of wealth and control because of all the Islamic faithful flooding into their country to visit the Kaaba. When millions and millions of Muslims are coming into the country, the wealth they leave behind makes the Saudis the dominate player in Islam because of their control of the Kaaba.

These are some of the things that place the nation of Saudi Arabia at risk of war amongst all other Muslim nations. In order to protect themselves, the Saudis have spent vast amounts of their financial resources on military hardware. They have some of the most advanced weapon systems in the world but their army is relatively small and not well trained. The leaders of their army have excellent political connections and affiliations with the ruling house of Saud, but this does

---

32   Joel Richardson, "Mystery Babylon, Unlocking the Bible's Greatest Prophetic Mystery," (WND Books, Washington DC, 2017) p. 261

not make them the most efficient fighting force. How Saudi Arabia would fare in an all-out conflict remains to be seen. If what we have seen in our study of biblical patterns is any indication, then Mecca and the ruling family of the house of Saud are going to be annihilated by a coalition of Islamic countries led by the nation of Turkey in the not too distant future.

The Current Situation in Saudi Arabia

Almost inexplicably, Saudi Arabia has recently been implicated in the disappearance of a Turkish reporter inside the Saudi Arabian consulate in Istanbul. A Turkish citizen, reporter Jamal Khashoggi, a reporter critical of the Saudi government, entered the Saudi consulate in order to obtain a wedding document and was never heard from again. The Washington Post reported that Khashoggi was likely killed by a team of 15 Saudi nationals that dismembered his body and removed it from the Saudi consulate in boxes.[33]

President Erdogan of Turkey has said that the missing reporter was a friend of his and has called on the leader of Saudi Arabia, Muhammad bin Salman, to provide an explanation of what had happened to reporter Khashoggi after he entered the Saudi Embassy in Istanbul. President Erdogan has threatened repercussions if his missing friend is not accounted for.

In light of Saudi Arabia's current tenuous situation in the Islamic world, this act is almost like Saudi Arabia taking a stick and poking it in the eye of the beast waiting in Turkey. It certainly gives President Erdogan of Turkey ammunition for retaliation against Saudi Arabia in the future. It is not known

---

33   Erin Cunningham and Kareem Fahim, "Erdogan: Journalist's disappearance very, very, upsetting," Washington Post, October 8, 2018

how much it will take for Turkey to react militarily against future aggressive moves by the Saudis.

What is of the most interest to us is what is going to happen when Turkey becomes the eighth beast empire in the biblical pattern? What can we expect? What insights are given to us in the biblical pattern we have been studying? Let's take a look at that now.

CHAPTER TWELVE

The Emergence of the New Ottoman Empire

Everything as we know it is going to change when the new Ottoman Empire takes control of the Muslim world. We will describe some of those changes later but first let's concentrate on the clues that God's Word gives us. The man that arises to lead this empire had been described by God's Word as a very dark and sinister individual, with beast like characteristics. The beast is so intertwined with the new beast empire kingdom that they become almost one in their actions. We find a description given of the beast in Revelation:

> People worshiped the dragon because he had given authority to the beast, and they also worshiped the beast and asked, "Who is like the beast? Who can wage war against it?" The beast was given a mouth to utter proud words and blasphemies and to exercise its authority for forty-two months. It opened its mouth to blaspheme God, and to slander his name and his dwelling place and those who live in heaven. It was given power to wage war against God's holy people and to conquer them.

And it was given authority over every tribe, people, language and nation. All inhabitants of the earth will worship the beast—all whose names have not been written in the Lamb's book of life, the Lamb who was slain from the creation of the world. (Revelation 13:4-8 NIV)

There are some points we need to recognize about this passage. It says that the beast was given a mouth—the mouth is the leader of the beast kingdom who is constantly saying derisive and slanderous things about God. It also says that the beast is going to wage war with the saints of God and that he is going to overcome them. There is a reason that this is going to happen that we will get into later. It also says that the beast is going to rule over many tribes, peoples, languages and nations. He is going to be tremendously successful during his time of power. But one of the most important things this passage says is that he is going to exercise his authority for only 42 months or three and a half years. His time of power is limited by the Lord.

According to the passage we have just reviewed, a leader is going to rise in what we have identified in the biblical pattern as Turkey, and will assume a great position of power in the world and conquer and subdue many nations. There is only one person in the world at this time who is actively trying to bring the events of the biblical pattern to pass that will lead to the formation of the eighth beast empire. That leader is Recep Tayyip Erdogan. He has never disguised his intentions and has told the world many times that he is going to bring the Ottoman Empire back. His intention is to rule the world through the renewed Ottoman Empire. What else can we expect from President Erdogan of Turkey? Has he ever told us his intentions when he controls the Muslim world?

The Mind of the Beast

It is rare for us to ever know the true intentions of a man like President Erdogan. Looking back in history, many people would have really liked to have known what a man like Adolf Hitler had in mind when he rose to power in Germany. Then maybe his actions would not have surprised so many people because they would have been understood in advance. In a rare glimpse into the mind of a man who may soon unleash war and destruction on the entire world, President Erdogan spoke candidly to a newspaper controlled by his government in a recent interview. Perhaps not realizing that his words would soon be known to those outside of Turkey, President Erdogan of Turkey told the Turkish daily newspaper Yeni Safak of his vision for the future of Islam. He posed the following question: "What if an army of Islam was formed against Israel?"

President Erdogan then outlined the shocking details of his plan for the future. He stated that if all 57 members of the Organization of Islamic Cooperation (OIC) would join together to form an army, then they would have an army of Islam that would easily be able to overwhelm the nation of Israel and wipe the Jewish State off the map. He said, "Each day that Jerusalem is under occupation is an insult to us."[34] President Erdogan considers the land of Israel to be Islamic land and that the Jewish nation is an occupying force in Muslim lands.

---

34 Adam Eliyahu Berkowitz, "Will Turkey Lead An End-Of-Days Global Islamic Jihad Against Israel And The US?" BreakingIsraelNews, 12 March, 2018, https://www.breakingnewsisraelnews.com/104068/will-turkey-lead-an-end-of-days-global-islamic-jihad-against-isreal-and-the-us/#6h5a4MVrekmbhEwT.97

President Erdogan then provided the details for the assault. He said the combined forces of the Islamic states would form the largest army in the world with a combined total of 5,206,100 men. That is an army four times larger than all of the armed forces of the United States. His battle plans included the neutralization of the United States before the assault on Israel would take place although he didn't provide details on how this would occur. He then stated that Israel has a substantially inferior army of 160,000 with the entire population of the Jewish State at 8,049,314. Erdogan commented that the population of Istanbul alone exceeds 14 million people. He said that the combined might of the Islamic world could easily overwhelm the nation of Israel and remove the Jewish presence from the land that should only be composed of Muslims.[35]

Now we have a candid glimpse into the mind of the man resurrecting the Ottoman Empire in Turkey. He wants to destroy Israel. What Recep Tayyip Erdogan doesn't realize is that the Lord already knows the plans for a future assault against his chosen people. God knows the future leader's plans and has already prepared for a way to deal with this assault against His people. What President Erdogan doesn't know is that his plans to destroy Israel have already been depicted in God's Word. In one of the most detailed of the intersecting prophecies, the Lord has detailed what is going to happen when a huge army comes against the nation of Israel in the last days to destroy it. It is described in an intersecting prophecy to the beastly kingdom prophecy and is found in the writings of Ezekiel. The man leading the assault against God's people is given an interesting name. He is called Gog.

---

35   Ibid.

The Emergence of the New Ottoman Empire

Let's set the stage for the appearance of the man who would be Gog.

- At some point in the near future a strong leader from the nation of Turkey is going to bring back the Ottoman Empire, an empire that dominated and united the Muslim world for 500 years. That strong leader is most likely Recep Tayyip Erdogan, the President of the nation of Turkey.

- At the same time, the leadership arm of the Muslim religion, the Islamic Caliphate is going to be brought back to Turkey where it was headquartered for 500 years.

- The new Ottoman Empire and Caliphate are going to unite the entire Muslim world under their leadership.

- At some point in time, the city of Mecca is going to be destroyed and the ruling party in the nation of Saudi Arabia, the house of Saud, is going to be removed from power and Saudi Arabia will be controlled by Turkey.

- The new Ottoman Empire will have access to the combined military might of the entire coalition of Islamic States. In addition to an army of over five million men, they could possibly have access to biological and chemical weapons, as well as a means to procure nuclear weapons. This will make them the largest fighting force in the world and one of the most feared.

- President Erdogan and the new Ottoman Empire have plans to neutralize the United States so that it will not interfere in Erdogan's goal to attack and destroy the nation of Israel. How they will accomplish this has not been disclosed. In a later chapter we will discuss the United States and the biblical pattern impacting America and the possible fate awaiting us.
- The new leader of the Ottoman Empire will lead for 42 months or three and a half years.

The time that the new Ottoman Empire is in power will be an absolute hell on earth. The atrocities committed by the new leader will far exceed those committed by Adolf Hitler and the Nazis. So we don't doubt the capabilities of the new Ottoman Empire, let's remember what the old Ottoman Empire accomplished. It almost conquered the entire world. Here is a map showing the potential control of the new Ottoman Empire:

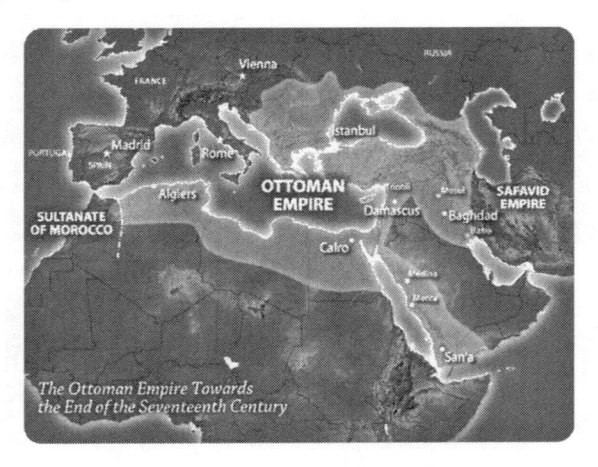

Not pictured are the most populated Islamic countries like Indonesia, India and Pakistan. This means that the new Islamic

Caliphate and Ottoman Empire will have control in nations in three separate continents—Africa, Europe, and Asia. They will have a fighting force that is impossible to ignore and will dictate their will to the rest of the world.

Near the end of the new leader's forty two month reign, he will launch an all-out attack against the nation of Israel. What follows next is the intersecting prophecy that describes the outcome of this massive army's intrusion in the land of Israel to annihilate the Jewish state, and wipe Israel off the face of the map. This intersecting prophecy has its own name. It is called the "Gog, Magog War" in God's Word and was described by the Prophet Ezekiel.

To those in the Islamic world, bent on the destruction of the tiny Jewish nation, the Gog/Magog war will become the "mother of all intersecting prophecies" and a warning they should have heeded.

CHAPTER THIRTEEN

The Gog, Magog War

What exactly is the war of Gog and Magog? Let's take a look at the passages describing this conflict now. The passages are found in Ezekiel. They describe a leader known as Gog and a massive army he brings into the land of Israel.

> Son of man, set your face against Gog, of the land of Magog, the chief prince of Meshek and Tubal; prophesy against him and say: I am against you, Gog, chief prince of Meshek and Tubal. I will turn you around, put hooks in your jaws and bring you out with your whole army—your horses, your horsemen fully armed, and a great horde with large and small shields, all of them brandishing their swords. Persia, Cush and Put will be with them, all with shields and helmets, also Gomer with all its troops, and Beth Togarmah from the far north with all its troops—the many nations with you. (Ezekiel 38:2-6 NIV)

Who is the mysterious Gog? And who are all of these other people listed in the passage? Where do they come from?

Gog is the name of the leader of this coalition of people coming against the land of Israel. The passage associates Gog with the land of Magog. Where is the land of Magog?

Magog was one of the sons of Japheth and Magog is the name of a people and an area where they settled. *The Moody Atlas of Bible Lands* can show us exactly where the land of Magog is located as we have seen once before.

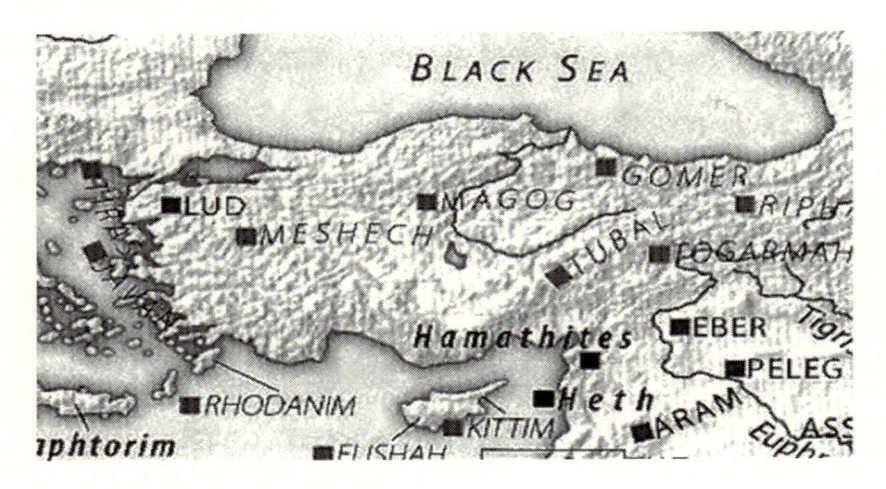

Magog is in the geographic center of the nation of Turkey. The reference to Magog is clearly pointing us to the modern day nation of Turkey. Gog is therefore a leader and the chief prince that arises from the land of Turkey. In other words, Gog is the leader that provides the impetus for the upcoming attack on Israel, and Gog has ties to Turkey for his power base. His power and authority come from Turkey because he is their chief prince and spokesman. The term "chief prince" is reserved for one that has control over the Caliphate in Islamic tradition. Not only is Gog the leader of the attacking armies, he is also the de-facto leader of the Caliphate.

What is truly astonishing is the link that Recep Tayyip Erdogan has with the beast that rises out of the sea in Revelation. President Erdogan was born in the land of Turkey and spent his young adulthood in the city of Rize on the Black Sea. Is it just a curious happenstance that President Erdogan grew to adulthood in Rize on the Black Sea, and the Book of Revelation depicts a "beast rising up out of the sea" that takes control of the final beast empire? Is this a biblical play on words? President Erdogan came from Rize on the Black Sea, and the biblical beast "rises" from the sea. Can this interplay of words be a mere coincidence or is there some deeper significance that the Lord is trying to get us to notice?

The Composition of the Attacking Army

The description of Gog and his army mentioned many names and places that you probably are not familiar with. In the map provided you can see that Meshech, Tubal, Magog, Gomer and Togarmah are all located in the modern day nation of Turkey. That means that five of the members of the attacking coalition listed in the passage are from the nation of Turkey. Turkey plays a major part in the future attack against the nation of Israel.

Let's look at the other members of the attacking nations. "Persia, Ethiopia and Libya with them, all of them with shield and helmet." (Ezekiel 38:5)

Persia is the modern day nation of Iran, and Ethiopia is what the biblical experts called the ancient land of "Cush," which is immediately south of Egypt in the land that is presently called Sudan. Sudan became the "Islamic Republic of Sudan" in 1989 and has become a hotbed of Islamic repression against Christianity and other religions since then. Libya is identified as

"Phut" and is the area west of Egypt in the modern day nation of Libya and includes small areas of Algeria and Tunisia also.

What do all of the attacking members of this coalition have in common? They are all Islamic. Turkey, Iran, Sudan, Libya, Algeria and Tunisia are all Muslim nations. The Muslim religion dominates all of their populations, cultures and institutions. They may all have separate and diverse cultures, but at their core they are completely controlled by the Islamic religion.

Let's list the aggressors in the Gog/Magog coalition and where they are from:

- Magog-Turkey
- Meshech-Turkey
- Tubal- Turkey
- Persia-Iran
- Ethiopia (Cush)-Sudan
- Libya (Phut)-Libya, parts of Algeria and Tunisia
- Gomer-Turkey
- Togarmah-Turkey

The Possible Motivation of the Gog/Magog Army

Gog is going to lead all of this coalition in an end time assault on the nation of Israel. There is a very important question we need to ask about how Gog is going to accomplish this feat. How does one motivate and unite an army of this size to come together with the defined goal of defeating and annihilating the nation of Israel?

Something must have happened that was so terrible in the eyes of the Muslim religion that it demands an overwhelming response. It must be an injustice so great that the Islamic leaders feel they must respond to maintain credibility. The retaliation must be this great so that it matches the seriousness of the alleged offense. What could possibly have happened?

In a masterstroke of deceptive manipulation, what if Gog was to blame the destruction of Mecca and the Kaaba on the nation of Israel and the Jewish people? An attack on the icon of the Islamic religion would demand a response such as we see in the Gog/Magog war. When Mecca is destroyed, in addition to the loss of life and property, an almost incalculable amount of wealth is going to disappear in an instant. All of the Muslim people will be demanding justice for the destruction of the sacred city and the crippling economic blow they have suffered. It would unite the Islamic world like nothing else.

From the description in Ezekiel, it seems that the main motivation of the massive army is to plunder and loot the land of Israel. It's almost as if looting the land of Israel is some sort of retribution for the loss of a massive amount of wealth. Let's look at the description of the motivation of the attacking army:

> I will plunder and loot and turn my hand against the resettled ruins and the people gathered from the nations, rich in livestock and goods, living at the center of the land. Sheba and Dedan and the merchants of Tarshish and all her villages will say to you, "Have you come to plunder? Have you gathered your hordes to loot, to carry off silver and gold, to take away livestock and goods and to seize much plunder?" (Ezekiel 38:12-13 NIV)

There is no doubt that the attacking army to coming to rob and steal. What is very curious are the ones asking if the army's motivation is to plunder and steal? Sheba, Dedan and the merchants of Tarshish are the ones asking the questions. Who are these enigmatic entities? The Bible identifies Dedan as the people living in Saudi Arabia south of the nation of Jordan. This would include the areas surrounding the city of Mecca. Sheba is the area in the southwestern corner of the Arabian Peninsula, south of Mecca and including Yemen. The merchants of Tarshish are the merchants carrying goods by land and sea for the Arabian people.

The ones asking the questions are those who were destroyed and devastated when Turkey attacked Mecca and Saudi Arabia. This is an important clue to the identity of the real attacker of Mecca. Israel was not the perpetrator of the destruction of Mecca, Turkey is the real party responsible for the annihilation of Mecca. It is subtle irony that the ones destroyed and devastated by Turkey are the ones questioning Gog when he comes to blame Israel for his own deeds. You blame who you want to blame in order to deflect attention from yourself. Gog will blame Israel for the destruction he inflicted on Mecca to justify his attack on the Jewish people.

The Fate of the Gog/Magog Army

When Gog comes to attack the Jewish people, he will be treating Israel as if it has no right to exist and that it should be wiped off the face of the earth. This has constantly been the position of the Muslim nations since the inception of Israel in May of 1948. With his massive army, Gog is now ready to accomplish the dream of the armies of Islam—the complete and total annihilation of the nation of Israel and the Jewish people.

What Gog and his hordes never counted on is the Lord's reaction to their invasion of His land to destroy His people. Gog is going to experience something few people have ever endured in our day and age. The Lord will tolerate many things in His infinite mercy, but He will not tolerate the total and wanton destruction of His people that have been gathered out of the nations into His land. The Lord is going to be furious with the invading army foolish enough to attack the land of His chosen people. Gog and his army are going to be decimated by the onslaught of the Lord in His anger. The following passage makes this clear in the Bible:

> This is what will happen in that day: When Gog attacks the land of Israel, my hot anger will be aroused, declares the Sovereign Lord. (Ezekiel 38:18 NIV)

The Lord is going to act to destroy Gog and his armies—and He is going to do it by supernatural intervention from Heaven. The Bible tells us this and describes exactly how He will accomplish the destruction of Gog and his armies. First the Bible tells us that there is going to be a cataclysmic earthquake—one so widespread that it will be felt by all the people on the face of the earth.

> For in my jealousy and in the fire of my wrath have I spoken, Surely in that day there shall be a shaking in the land of Israel, so that the fishes of the sea, and the fowls of the heaven, and the beasts of the field, and all creeping things that creep upon the earth, and the men that are upon the face of the earth, shall shake at my

presence, and the mountains shall be thrown down, and
the steep places shall fall, and every wall shall fall to the
ground. (Ezekiel 38:19-20)

This is not going to be a typical regional earthquake, but will be a worldwide earthquake felt by everyone living on the face of the earth. No one will be safe from this earthquake. It will impact "all men" and every fish, bird and creature on the face of the earth. It's as if the Lord is shaking the world to try to get our attention—to see if we will pay attention to what is going on. He will also be sending a message to Gog that he will not succeed.

What occurs next will be just as alarming. The Lord will use supernatural intervention to destroy Gog and all but one-sixth of his gigantic army. The Lord will be marshaling His weapons of destruction to accomplish His purpose. These weapons will come from the sky and the heavens and will pummel the earth and mountains where Gog's hordes are massing for their attack. The Bible tells us this in the following verse:

And I will plead against him with pestilence and with blood; and I will rain upon him, and upon his bands, and upon the many people that are with him, an overflowing rain, and great hailstones, fire, and brimstone. (Ezekiel 38:22)

What are the great hailstones, fire and brimstone that the Lord is talking about in this passage? This passage is not talking about normal rain that we are familiar with. Instead, what is being described is a more appropriate description of meteorites and volatile materials falling from the skies and igniting a conflagration in the fire that ensues. How can something falling from the sky do that?

It's not as difficult as it might seem when we consider the materials existing in space in our solar system or the materials comprising the interstellar medium. This is a rain that is comprised of volatile materials that are routinely found in the interstellar medium and can be brought into our solar system by a large object passing through space.

Astronomers have done an extensive analysis of the interstellar medium and have found an abundance of complex volatile materials that exist in space. In fact, almost half of the substances found in space will burn when combined with oxygen and a spark to ignite them.[36] If any of those volatile materials were to come into contact with the atmosphere of earth, all you would need is some oxygen and a spark and you could ignite an inferno. There would be literal sheets of fire falling from the skies. The atmosphere supplies the oxygen, and the spark could come from meteors as they become red-hot and streak across the sky.

This, or something like it, may be what the Lord meant when He describes the abnormal rain, fire, hailstones and brimstone that fall from the sky to engulf Gog and his hordes. The Lord reinforces this point when He says in Ezekiel 39:6: "And I will send a fire on Magog."

The Lord does not depend on man to accomplish His will. In the case of Gog and his hordes, He will use materials that are readily available to Him from His creation in the interstellar and solar medium. The Lord's weapons that He has available to Him in space will be the means to accomplish the destruction

---

36 Carl Sagan, Ann Druyan, Comet, (New York, NY: Pocket Books, 1985,) pp. 150-151

of Gog and his massive army. This follows a pattern that the Lord has used in the past to accomplish His purpose.

Another Biblical Pattern Surfaces

The method the Lord uses to accomplish His purposes is usually very different from what we would imagine. If God wants to intervene in a situation, He certainly does not need to depend on man to fulfill His will. For example, we are given a description in the Bible of a way that the Lord used to carry out His supernatural intervention. The description given sounds very similar to the way the Lord will intervene in the Gog/Magog War.

> The noise of a multitude in the mountains, like as of a great people; a tumultuous noise of the kingdoms of nations gathered together: The Lord of Hosts mustereth the host of the battle. They come from a far country, from the end of heaven, even the Lord, and the weapons of his indignation, to destroy the whole land. Howl ye; for the day of the Lord is at hand; it shall come as a destruction from the Almighty. (Isaiah 13:4-6)

There are several observations we can make from this passage. First, the Lord is using an army gathered from the "end of heaven." Second, the weapons of His indignation come from heaven and will destroy the land. Third, the weapons of the Lord are deployed against multitudes in the mountains, against many people and nations gathered together. Fourth, when the Lord strikes, it will "come as a destruction from the Almighty."

Has there been any time in the past when the Lord has used supernatural heavenly intervention to destroy an army that has come against His people? Yes, there is an example in God's Word of just such an occurrence. Let's look at that example now because it establishes another biblical pattern that we need to be aware of.

The Supernatural Intervention Pattern

The Lord has used people many times in the past to accomplish His will. The scriptures are filled with examples of this. There are times the Lord makes a point of not using man or anything that man can do to fulfill His purposes. There was an example in ancient Israel of just such an occurrence; where the Lord used supernatural intervention to protect His people. It happened when an arrogant and prideful leader of the Assyrians named Sennacherib came against the Jewish people surrounded in Jerusalem. He brought a huge army of 185,000 men with him and laid siege to the city of Jerusalem with the intent on destroying the Jewish people.

The King of Judah at that time was a man named Hezekiah. King Hezekiah realized the predicament of the Jewish people and turned to God for help. He repented of his sins, and then implored all the people of Jerusalem to repent and turn back to God. The people listened to Hezekiah, humbled themselves, and turned away from the things that were alienating them from God. The Lord moved to save His people by destroying the army of Sennacherib in one night.

> Behold, I will send a blast upon him...Then the angel of the Lord went forth, and smote in the camp of the Assyrians a hundred and four-score and five thousand: and when they arose early in the morning, behold, they were all dead corpses. (Isaiah 37:7, 36)

The Lord used his heavenly agents and supernatural intervention to destroy an army of 185,000 Assyrians laying siege to the city of Jerusalem in one night. The Lord established in this biblical pattern that He can and will intervene against an army that is formed to destroy His people. The Gog/Magog war will be another example of a biblical pattern where the Lord intervenes through supernatural means to protect His land and people.

The End of Gog

The massive army that Gog has raised and used to attack the nation of Israel will be destroyed. There will only be a sixth part of it left. "And I will turn thee back, and leave but the sixth part of thee." (Ezekiel 39:2)

Gog's fate will be equally as devastating:

> Then I will strike your bow from your left hand and make your arrows drop from your right hand. On the mountains of Israel you will fall, you and all your troops and the nations with you. I will give you as food to all kinds of carrion birds and to the wild animals. You will fall in the open field, for I have spoken, declares the Sovereign Lord. (Ezekiel 39:3-5 NIV)

The majority of the vast army that Gog has brought into the land of Israel and Gog himself will die when the Lord intervenes in this battle. There is an interesting phrase used before Gog is killed. It says the Lord will "strike your bow from your left hand." An interesting parallel is that the first horseman of the apocalypse, the rider on the white horse, will have a bow in his hand, and he will go forth conquering and to conquer just like Gog. (Revelation 6:2)

Gog and his multitudes will be buried in Israel in the valley of Hamon-gog.

> And it shall come to pass in that day, that I will give unto Gog a place there of graves in Israel, the valley of the passengers on the east of the sea; and it shall stop the noses of the passengers: and there shall they bury Gog and all his multitude: and they shall call it the valley of Hamon-gog." (Ezekiel 39:11)

Gog will die in this battle and be buried in a grave in Israel. Gog has met his fate and can no longer wreak havoc on the world. He can no longer wage war on a global scale; his war machine will no longer cause famines to sweep across the world, and he will no longer be able to unleash pestilence that will decimate the world's population.

Gog will be gone, but now we are faced with a perplexing dilemma. Who is the man of sin or the "antichrist" as we have come to know him that will rise up in his place? Is he the same man as Gog or is it a different person that rises up to take Gog's place? Does the biblical pattern foretell and predict that another man will rise up and assume control of the eighth beast empire?

There is a lot of confusion surrounding these issues. What if we were to tell you that the subtle pattern of two is going to reassert itself in the end-times landscape, and another leader twice as bad as Gog will emerge on the world scene? And what if we were to tell you that all of the details about this second person were carefully inserted into the biblical pattern? Would this be something that you would want to know?

Not only would we need to know these details, but it would be imperative that we understand them. We can unlock what we need to know in the biblical pattern and the "tale of two antichrists."

CHAPTER FOURTEEN

The Tale of Two Antichrists

One of the things that the Apostle John told us was that in the last times there would be many antichrists that would come. In fact, John said that because of the many antichrists in the world, we would know that it is the last times. "Ye have heard that antichrist shall come, even now are there many antichrists; whereby we know that it is the last time." (1 John 2:18)

What may be surprising to many is the fact that the Bible clearly describes two different leaders that can best be described as beasts arising to lead the end-time beast empire. The first beast "rises up out of the sea" (Revelation 13:1) and the second beast comes up out of the earth. "And I beheld another beast coming up out of the earth…" (Revelation 13:11) The second beast rises to power after the first beast has dominated the earth for forty two months.

There is no ambiguity in what the Bible is saying, but there is a tremendous amount of confusion surrounding the two beasts because we don't recognize what the Bible is telling us.

We have been told by the books and literature published in our day that the antichrist is killed, but then comes back to life. We have been told that the antichrist receives a head wound so severe that it kills him, but then it is healed. We have been told that there is only one antichrist—but that one antichrist is really the two antichrists described in Revelation. We have been told these things so many times that we have come to accept these opinions without questioning them. We have given up trying to resolve the supposed contradictions without digging deeper to see if we can discover what the Bible is really trying to tell us.

These things may be what we have been told—but this is not what the biblical pattern asserts. The Bible and the biblical pattern clearly predict that there will be two different antichrists. If that is the case, and there is a second antichrist, then the Bible should provide a storyline for the second antichrist—just as the biblical pattern showed us the storyline for the eighth beast empire and its leader, the first antichrist, known as Gog. The second antichrist will have his own story and it will be revealed in another biblical pattern.

There are two different stories, two different fates, told in two different places in the Bible. There will be many similar circumstances in each story, but it is the story of two different individuals.

Let's take a look at the overview of the two different stories. **In one, an empire is gone and then comes back. In the other, a man is gone and then comes back**. Both an empire and a man are gone and then come back—this is the path of the two different antichrists.

We have already told the story of the empire that was gone and then is going to come back. It was revealed in the biblical pattern of the beastly kingdoms. The Ottoman Empire was disbanded after the conclusion of the First World War. It will reemerge on the world scene when the man who will be Gog brings it back in the near future. This is the story of the empire that will be gone but then will reappear and the first antichrist.

The man who is gone but will come back is the second antichrist and he is far more difficult for us to recognize. The Bible gives us an important clue in Revelation where it tells us that he "comes up out of the earth." (Revelation 13:11) So we are looking for a man that comes up out of the earth and will rise to control the entire world after the defeat of a powerful Islamic leader (Gog). To most Christians this is an enigmatic clue that gives us very little to go on. Most Muslims would not be able to tell you the identity of the man in question either. However, to Shiite Muslims, this is all they need to know to provide you with name of the mysterious man in question and the location from which he will emerge out of the earth. This almost sounds unbelievable but it is undeniably true. In order to understand this, there are things that we need to know about the Islamic religion and some background we need to become familiar with also.

The Two Branches of the Islamic Religion

We need to understand that there has been a war going on since the time of Muhammad's death between the two main branches of the Islamic religion—the Sunni and the Shia. Muhammad, the founder of the Islamic religion, died in 632 AD without naming a successor. After his death a strong leader arose to take control of the Muslim world. His name was Abu Bakr and he assumed the role of the first caliph (successor). The caliph is the leader of the Caliphate (Islam under the rule of a caliph). Abu Bakr ruled until 661 AD and after his death a civil war broke out between the Shia and Sunni branches of Islam. There were two different philosophies on the proper governance for all of Islam. The Sunnis felt that the strongest leader should prevail and become the caliph, and the Shiites believed that only a direct descendant of Muhammad should become the leader. The Shiites called their leader the Imam (one who walks in front).

The Sunni branch of Islam emerged as the stronger of the two branches of Islam, and the caliphs soon began to dominate the Muslim world. They sought to suppress the voices of a different direction for Islam expressed by the Shiite Imams. The Sunnis felt there could only be one true leader in Islam, and so they began the systematic extermination of the dissenting voice of the Shiite Imams. From the first Imam, to the eleventh Imam, all were killed by the Sunnis on orders from the Caliphate. Most of the Imams were poisoned, and one was killed in battle against the Caliphate and then beheaded.[37]

This led to the widespread oppression of the Shiite minority. Their Imams were killed by the Sunni Caliphate and their voices were suppressed by the ruling Sunni branch of Islam. The Shiites felt that they were a persecuted branch of the Muslim world, and all their hopes could only reside in the coming of an Imam that is destined to lead the world. He will

---

[37] Wikipedia, "Imamah (Shia Doctrine)," http://en.wikipedia.org/wiki/Imamah_(Shia_doctrine).

be known as the Twelfth Imam. Here is some background information on the future Twelfth Imam.

The Twelfth Imam

His father was the eleventh Imam, Hasan al-Askari. He was an Imam that was dominated by the Abbasid Caliphate and was imprisoned in Samarra, Iraq.[38] The Abbasid Caliphates were from Iraq and derived their name from the uncle of Muhammad named Abbas. The Sunni Caliphate kept tight control over the eleventh Imam, so much so that he sent his son into hiding in order to protect him. He didn't want his son to be controlled by the interference of the Caliphate, so he secreted him away and the son disappeared from Samarra, Iraq where his father was being held captive by the Sunni Caliphate.

The son who was secreted away and disappeared is known as the Twelfth Imam. He was born on July 29th, 868 or 869 AD (two different dates are given for the year of his birth). While the one that will be known as the Twelfth Imam was still a young child, he is said to have gone into occultation (hiding), and is due to reappear on the world scene after the Sunni controlled Caliphate suffers a tremendous defeat in the end-times of the Islamic religion. The Twelfth Imam went into occultation (hiding) in 872 AD, and devout Shiite Muslims have been awaiting his promised return ever since that time.[39]

The common belief among followers of the Twelfth Imam (which is primarily modern day Iran), is that the Twelfth Imam is going to come out of occultation (hiding) when the Sunni Muslim Caliphate has suffered a defeat so cataclysmic that it

---
38 Ibid
39 Ibid

will rock the entire Islamic world to its core. This defeat will be so catastrophic that the Sunni Muslims will be devastated and unable to rule due to the loss of their leaders and armies. The time will then be right, during the aftermath of war and pandemonium, for the appearance of the long awaited Twelfth Imam. It is at that time that he will emerge to bring order and peace to a world in total chaos and disorder.

If you ask any of the Shiite faithful they can tell you exactly where the long awaited Twelfth Imam will come from—it is deep in the ground. It is a specific place where the faithful anticipate his arrival. It is said that he will emerge from a deep well in the ground—and this place is so sacred to the Shiite Muslims that they have built a mosque around it. It is called the Jamkaran Mosque and it is in the modern day nation of Iran. Here is a picture of that mosque:

Inside this structure is a deep well that goes down into the earth. This "well" is the place from which the Twelfth Imam is going to reappear according to Shiite scholars. He will somehow rise up out of the earth, and his appearance will be witnesses by many and will send shock waves across the Islamic community. We do not know the process by which he will appear. It most likely involves some sort of dark ritual. Medical technology has advanced to the point where a cloning process may be involved, we simply do not know. The process will probably involve an occultist ritual since the hiding process was called occultation. However they manage it, one claiming to be the Twelfth Imam will emerge from the well and appear to the world.

What is the name of the Twelfth Imam that will arise from the well inside the Jamkaran Mosque—the son who was secreted away by his father to arise again in times of trouble for the Islamic religion? It is Muhammad al-Mahdi. His full name is Muhammad ibn al-Hasan al-Mahdi, but most will know him simply as the "Mahdi." He has many titles that he is known by in the Shiite branch of Islam. They are "The Guided One," the "Hidden Imam," "The Proof," the "Lord of our Times," the "One Vested with Divine Authority," "God's Remainder," and "The One Who Will Rise and Fill the Universe with Justice."[40]

What is very interesting is how the emergence of the "Mahdi" from deep inside the earth correlates with the appearance of the second beast in the Book of Revelation. The second beast comes up out of the earth in a scene that foreshadows something ominous. "And I beheld another beast coming up out of the earth; and he had two horns like a lamb, and he spake as a dragon." (Revelation 13:11) The second beast comes up out of the earth—in the exact manner the Mahdi makes his appearance to the world—rising up from the Jamkaran well in Iran. The correlation between these two appearances is uncanny.

What is even more astounding is that the Book of Revelation further clarifies this event by describing the entity that ascends from the bottomless pit as being one that had previously lived, and then was not, and yet somehow lives again.

---

40 Ibid

"The beast that thou sawest was and is not; and shall ascend out of the bottomless pit, and go into perdition: and they that dwell on the earth shall wonder, whose names were not written in the book of life from the foundation of the world, when they behold the beast that was, and is not, and yet is." (Revelation 17:8)

The first beast of Revelation 13 symbolizes an empire that was gone and then comes back with a leader that reigns for forty-two months, and the second beast symbolizes a man that was gone and comes back and rules the beast kingdom resurrected by the first leader for another forty-two months.

A Summary of Important Points

Let's summarize what we have just discussed and review the information we have learned from Islamic history and the biblical pattern to see what the Bible is trying to tell us.

- The biblical pattern tells us that the Ottoman Empire will be reestablished on the earth after having been disbanded in 1924.
- A powerful man that comes from Turkey will arise to bring back the Ottoman Empire.
- The powerful leader from Turkey is called Gog by the Bible. The only man that fits the profile of this enigmatic leader today is Recep Tayyip Erdogan of Turkey.
- Gog will unite the Islamic world like no other modern Islamic leader and will unleash war, famine, pestilence and destruction that have not

been seen since the days of Adolf Hitler and the Third Reich.

- Gog will rule for 42 months or three and a half years after he reestablishes the Ottoman Empire.
- Toward the end of his rule, Gog will amass an Islamic army to annihilate the nation of Israel and the Jewish people.
- When he attacks Israel, Gog and all but one sixth of his army will be destroyed by supernatural intervention from heaven on the plains and mountains of Israel.
- Gog and his hordes will be buried in Israel. The process of burying the remainder of his army will take seven months because of the massive size of the army that was destroyed.
- Gog will be the first leader of the beast empire spoken of in Revelation 13.
- The second leader of the beast empire rises out of the earth around the time Gog and his army have suffered a devastating defeat in the Gog/Magog battle.
- Coinciding with the biblical prophecy of a leader rising out of the earth, there is a Shiite Hadith (teachings by Islamic scholars) depicting an end time leader arising from a well inside the Jamkaran Mosque in Iran after the Islamic world has suffered a tremendous defeat.
- The name of this leader is Muhammad ibn al-Hasan al-Mahdi, or the "Mahdi" and he is the

long awaited Twelfth Imam—the one promised to return by the Shiite branch of Islam.

- The Mahdi will end up ruling the entire world according to Shiite Islamic tradition and the profile given of the second leader in Revelation 13.
- The Mahdi or Twelfth Imam that rises to lead the Islamic beast empire after the death of Gog will fit the profile of the antichrist that Christians have been expecting since the Book of Revelation was written.

This summarizes many of the important points we have discussed so far. If the Mahdi or Twelfth Imam is the second beast leader arising in Revelation 13, then he must have is own storyline in the Bible. This storyline or biblical pattern depicting him will be similar to the beastly kingdom prophecies but different slightly. His story will be similar but unique. Let's take a look at the subtle difference in the clues given about the identity of the second leader.

What may be surprising to many is the fact that the Prophet Daniel describes a leader arising in the last days that possesses the characteristics of the awaited Twelfth Imam of the Shiite Muslims. Let's take a look at that now.

Daniel's Vision of the Four Beast Kingdoms

The Prophet Daniel had a vision of four beastly kingdoms and recorded what he saw:

> Four great beasts, each different from the others, came up out of the sea. The first was like a lion, and it had the

wings of an eagle. I watched until its wings were torn off and it was lifted from the ground so that I stood on two feet like a human being, and the mind of a human was given to it. And there before me was a second beast, which looked like a bear. It was raised up on one of its sides, and it had three ribs in its mouth between its teeth. It was told, "Get up and eat your fill of flesh!" After that, I looked, and there before me was another beast, one that looked like a leopard. And on its back it had four wings like those of a bird. This beast had four heads, and it was given authority to rule. (Daniel 7:3-6 NIV)

Let's describe was Daniel was seeing. The lion was symbolic of the Babylonian Empire as we discussed before in the beastly kingdom pattern. The bear is symbolic of the Medo-Persian Empire. The leopard was symbolic of the Grecian Empire and the four heads were the four generals that split up the empire after the death of Alexander the Great. The four generals were Cassander, Lysimachus, Seleucus, and Ptolemy. What Daniel is describing is consistent with three of the beastly kingdoms in the beastly kingdom biblical pattern.

There is something that is different about the description of the beastly kingdoms however. The difference is consistent with the rise of the little horn that Daniel describes next. Daniel describes a little horn that comes up amongst the three beast kingdoms and then overthrows three of them. Daniel described it this way:

> While I was thinking about the horns, there before me was another horn, a little one, which came up among them; and three of the first horns were uprooted before

it. This horn had eyes like the eyes of a human being, and a mouth that spoke boastfully. (Daniel 7:8 NIV)

We will discuss the three horns that will be removed in a later chapter, but the arrival of the little horn is different then we have seen before and the description of the beastly kingdoms is different. For example, the lion, symbolic of Babylon, has wings on it. Why would the lion, the symbol of the Babylonian Empire—located in modern day Iraq, have the wings of an eagle on it?

To gain proper perspective and insight into the symbols used, we need to remember the time frame Daniel is viewing in his vision. He is seeing the little horn or antichrist in his vision. The antichrist rises in the end times. Daniel is seeing these Islamic kingdoms in modern times, in our days, not in the times of the past. This is made clear by the symbols Daniel uses. Babylon was in what in now modern day Iraq. If you look at Iraq in our days, modern times, you would see the military presence of the United States. What is the symbol of the United States? It is the eagle. The US is so heavily invested militarily in Iraq that it seems that our country's eagle's wings are sprouting out of the back of the Babylonian lion. This is what Daniel is seeing—an end time Iraq with the dominating presence of the US military. The fact that the eagle's wings were torn off means that the United States is soon going to leave.

The Fourth Beast Kingdom in Daniel's Vision

Daniel's vision of the fourth beast kingdom must be a power that is in control when the little horn or antichrist arises. That means that the fourth beast kingdom he is seeing is most likely the renewed Ottoman Empire. Daniel hints at this when he describes the fourth beast kingdom:

> After that, in my vision at night I looked, and there before me was a fourth beast—terrifying and frightening and very powerful. It had large iron teeth; it crushed and devoured its victims and trampled underfoot whatever was left. It was different from all the former beasts, and it had ten horns. (Daniel 7:7 NIV)

Daniel states implicitly that this fourth beast "was different from all the former beasts." That means that this is not the Roman Empire, or the Eastern leg of the Roman Empire, but a new empire that has control over Islamic armies. In fact, it was so important to clarify that this beast empire was different than all the others that Daniel stated this important point two more times in his vision. "Then I wanted to know the meaning of the fourth beast, which was different from all the others and most terrifying…" (Daniel 7:19 NIV) "He gave me this explanation: The fourth beast is a fourth kingdom that will appear on earth. It will be different from all the other kingdoms and will devour the whole earth, trampling it down and crushing it." (Daniel 7:23 NIV)

From the clues we are given by Daniel, we can conclude the following about this fourth beast kingdom:

1. The fourth beast kingdom is an Islamic kingdom or empire that will be in power at the time the little horn or antichrist arises to take power.

2. All the components of this kingdom listed by Daniel are Islamic nations. This kingdom is an end time united Islamic empire.

3. Daniel states three times in his vision that this kingdom will be different from all the other kingdoms because it will conquer the entire earth, crush it and trample it down. No Islamic kingdom in the past has conquered the whole earth. No Islamic empire in the past has had access to weapons systems that will enable it to destroy millions upon millions of people with relative ease.

4. There will be ten horns or leaders in this end time Islamic empire.

5. Another leader, different from the others, a little horn will arise and subdue three leaders or kings.

6. The little horn will then take over this fourth beast kingdom, the end time Islamic empire and this empire will fulfill its destiny to rule and control the entire world.

The only empire this could possibly be is a new Ottoman Empire. This end time super empire is resurrected by Gog and then later controlled by the antichrist, the little horn of Daniel. Under these two leaders the people of the world are going to suffer as they never have before. Gog will represent the Sunni branch of this empire, and the antichrist will represent the Shiite branch of this last day's kingdom. This is the tale of the two antichrists. Each has his own storyline, and both have different biblical patterns describing them and what we can expect when they take power. We have touched on some of the things we can expect when Gog takes power, but we really haven't examined them in detail. Let's examine in detail what Gog will do when he takes over the new Ottoman Empire—this will better prepare us for the onslaught of the antichrist and what we can expect from the little horn.

CHAPTER FIFTEEN

The Devastating Legacy of Gog

Gog is going to leave a lasting imprint on the landscape of the entire world. He will fundamentally change many things during the time he is in power. His reign is so climactic that it begs the following question. Is Gog portrayed in any other area of the Bible beside the references in Ezekiel? Let's dig a little deeper in the Bible and see what further insights we can gain with our examination.

In Ezekiel, Gog is characterized as a leader with a bow in his left hand. (Ezekiel 39:3) Is there any other place in the Bible that refers to a leader with a "bow" in his hand? There is! It is found in Revelation:

> I watched as the Lamb opened the first of the seven seals. Then I heard one of the four living creatures say in a voice like thunder, "Come!" I looked and there before me was a white horse! Its rider held a bow, and he was given a crown, and he rode out as a conqueror bent on conquest. (Revelation 6:1-2 NIV)

Let's take a closer look at the symbols employed so we can understand what this verse is trying to tell us. First, a leader on a white horse is described. The white horse is symbolic of leadership. We find this reference in Revelation when Jesus Christ is depicted as coming from heaven riding upon a white horse. (Revelation 19:11) The leader riding on the white horse with a bow in his hand is a leader of an empire that is trying to conquer the world. He is given a crown—which denotes supreme leadership. This is exactly what will happen when Gog takes over the renewed Ottoman Empire. He will then proceed to lead his Islamic forces in an attempted subjugation of the entire world.

The leader depicted as having a bow in his left hand fits Gog perfectly. No other leader in end time prophecies is described as having a bow in his left hand. The leader described in the first seal of Revelation is none other than Gog. He is the leader on the white horse and is one of the four horsemen of the Apocalypse. He goes forth bent on conquering the world. The natural consequences of his actions are described by the other three horsemen of the Apocalypse.

The second horseman is described as riding a fiery red horse. He is depicted as unleashing war on a global scale.

> When the Lamb opened the second seal, I heard the second living creature say "Come!" Then another horse came out, a fiery red one. Its rider was given power to take peace from the earth and to make men slay each other. To him was given a large sword. (Revelation 6:3-4 NIV)

The Devastating Legacy of Gog

Gog's desire to rule the entire world will unleash war like we have not seen since the previous two World Wars. Peace will be taken from the earth when Gog leads his forces to carry out jihad on all nations that will not follow his leadership. He will have the combined forces of all the Islamic nations at his disposal to carry out his desires. Any nations not bending to his leadership will be attacked. War will be unleashed on a global scale.

The third horseman is a natural result of the first two. Famines so large they engulf the whole world spread throughout the globe. When people are worried about being killed in a war, they don't plant and grow crops like they normally would. Also, what limited crops are planted can be destroyed when the war continues unabated. Consequently, it is going to cost a whole day's wages just to be able to buy what a person needs for food for that day. We are told this in the following verses in the Bible.

> When the lamb opened the third seal, I heard the third living creature say "Come!" I looked, and there before me was a black horse! Its rider was holding a pair of scales in his hand. Then I heard what sounded like a voice among the four living creatures, saying, "A quart of wheat for a day's wages, and three quarts of barley for a day's wages, and do not damage the oil and wine." (Revelation 6:5-6 NIV)

Famine will overwhelm the entire world. There will not be enough food to go around and many people will die from starvation during the wars Gog unleashes on the world. It will be a horrible time to endure.

The last horseman summarizes some of our worst fears. This horseman rides a pale horse which is indicative of death. In fact, this rider's name is death. He will bring death on the world on a global scale from war, famine and plague; and by the wild beasts of the earth. He is described in the following manner:

> When the lamb opened the fourth seal, I heard the voice of the fourth living creature say, "Come!" I looked, and there before me was a pale horse! Its rider was named Death, and Hades was following close behind him. They were given power over a fourth of the earth to kill by sword, famine and plague, and by the wild beasts of the earth. (Revelation 6:7-8 NIV)

One of the most disturbing things about this description is the fact that one fourth of the world's population will be killed during this time. The current world's population is 7.3 billion people. That means that a little over 1.8 billion people are going to die during the time when the horsemen are released. That's more people than died during WW1 and WW2. Those 1.8 billion people will die during the wars, famines and plagues that devastate the world. The wild beasts of the earth can also refer to biological weapons. The world's arsenals contain many examples of biological weapons, and it is almost certain that some of these biological weapons will be used in this war. We can expect to see many horrendous diseases rampaging across the planet—all of them engineered to kill as many people as possible. Viable vaccines will be scarce and limited to those that release these diseases. One unchecked pandemic can easily kill millions upon millions of people.

The Devastating Legacy of Gog

It is a foregone conclusion that Gog will have access to biological weapons as well as nuclear and chemical weapons. Pakistan is an Islamic country that possesses nuclear weapons and will be a part of the coalition of nations that Gog controls. Whether they use these weapons remains to be seen. In the past, the despotic rulers of the world have used all weapons at their disposal to achieve their goals. Gog will probably be no different than the others.

Gog's legacy will be one of tremendous death and destruction during his reign as leader of the new Ottoman Empire. He will responsible for more deaths than we can possibly imagine. It is little wonder that he is assigned a place of death on the mountains of Israel when he leads a coalition of nations to attack Israel in the Gog/Magog war. The bow of war will be struck out of his left hand and he will die because of the hell he has unleashed on earth.

The problem is that Gog is not the only diabolical leader that will assume control of the coalition of nations that Gog has gathered from the Islamic world. Another leader will be waiting to take over what remains of the Islamic coalition as soon as Gog has been killed. Only this time, the world will open its arms to embrace the new ruler that appears on the scene. How can this possibly happen? How can the world be so deceived that they will openly accept a leader that will eventually be known as the antichrist? What misconceptions can lead to this grievous error? That is the topic of our next chapter.

CHAPTER SIXTEEN

The False Time of Peace

One of the biggest oversights of our generation is the failure to recognize the biblical patterns that the Lord has placed in the Bible and to avoid being deceived by the events happening around us. Because we are unfamiliar with these patterns, we are ill prepared to recognize the significance of the events occurring during these critical end time manifestations. Things of tremendous importance will be happening and many of us will be completely unaware of their significance. We will be looking for different things to happen because of what we have been told in popular books and teachings about the end times.

For example, if people were told that a huge battle takes place in the nation of Israel and a gigantic army composed of many nations was destroyed in this battle by intervention from the Lord; what would almost everyone tell you this battle was called? Almost anyone questioned would tell you that this was the Battle of Armageddon. Therein lays the problem. What is almost everyone expecting to happen after the Battle of Armageddon?

We have been told that Jesus Christ appears on the world scene after the cataclysmic annihilation in Armageddon. In fact, the Book of Revelation depicts Jesus Christ coming down from heaven on a white horse leading his army to destroy the armies of the antichrist. During this apocalyptic battle, Jesus Christ will appear to the world to usher in the greatest time of peace that this world has ever known. Everyone expects this. This is something we have all been told since the time we became Christians. It is a time we all look forward to.

This however is also the time when the devil will be able to create one of the greatest deceptions in the history of the world. Because we will confuse the Gog/Magog battle with the Battle of Armageddon, we will be open to deception. The Gog/Magog war is one battle in the last days—but it is not the final end time battle. Gog is an end time ruler, but he is not the only end time ruler that will have the characteristics of the antichrist. Because we have become conditioned to expect only one great end times battle, and only one antichrist to lead the forces of opposition—then anyone who appears and calls themselves Christ, after a devastating battle where armies have been destroyed by miraculous means, will be received with open arms. They will be accepted as the Messiah even if the doctrine they are teaching seems a little off. That person will be worshipped and accepted like no other person in the history of the world. He will be accepted by all religions on the face of the earth.

A false Messiah will appear, and if you don't accept the person who is claiming to be Christ at that time—then you will be labeled a malcontent and a trouble maker—someone who needs to be eliminated. People will think they are doing the world a great service if you are killed because they don't know

The False Time of Peace

the person claiming to be Christ is not Jesus Christ at all, but an impostor. Imagine the tragic dilemma you would be in if something like this happened.

According to the biblical pattern we have been studying, this is precisely what is going to happen. People are going to mistake the Gog/Magog war for the Battle of Armageddon with tragic consequences. They are also going to believe that Gog is the only antichrist, and that when he is eliminated then Christ will appear to lead all the nations of the world. The false Messiah will promise peace to the entire world, and the world will be more than ready to accept this false peace because of the terrible wars that have been devastating the world. The jubilation the world feels will be equivalent to the joy felt by all people when World War Two ended.

There will be a willing suspension of disbelief even when the one claiming to be Christ starts to do things that Jesus Christ would never do. This false Messiah will demand that those who will not worship him should be killed. This is a red flag that will be ignored at the time. This false Messiah will then claim that Christianity is not really the belief system we should be embracing—that the Islamic religion is where the real truth is found. This is a gospel other than the one taught in the Bible—a false gospel, but this will be ignored also. Then finally the antichrist will do something that is such a red flag that no one will be able to ignore it. He will demand that people take the mark of the beast, and that no one can buy or sell unless they have the mark of the antichrist. This is a line that Christians know they can't cross and a red flag they can't ignore. If you take the mark of the beast you will be declaring your allegiance to this false Messiah and will be denying Jesus Christ. This will permanently cut you off from the saving grace of Jesus Christ and will place you in the camp of those that follow the antichrist.

If you have a heart of darkness, you can only hide it for so long before people begin to see you for who you really are. Your true nature will eventually reveal itself. This is what is going to happen with the false Messiah who is actually the little horn of Daniel—the antichrist—he will hide his true nature but only for a set amount of time.

The way this type of falsehood can be foisted upon people is by general ignorance of what the Bible is actually trying to tell us. We need to realize that there is more than one end time war in the biblical pattern—we need to recognize which war it actually is by who is leading the armies and the composition of the armies involved. The battle of Armageddon is not the only last day's battle where the Lord intervenes to accomplish His will. If we call every end time war the Battle of Armageddon then we are setting ourselves up for deception.

The same reasoning applies to both of the antichrists. We need to realize when the Lord defeats the coalition of nations coming against His people, He is going to defeat both branches of Islam, the Sunni and the Shiites, and both of their versions of end time leaders that arise to oppose Him. Gog is the leader of the Sunni branch of Islam, and the little horn or antichrist is the leader of the Shiite branch of Islam. If you defeat just one, you have not defeated the more dangerous second antichrist. It's the subtle pattern of two reasserting itself in the biblical pattern again. The Shiite antichrist will have to be defeated also to have the final victory over the beast empire.

The False Time of Peace

In the previous chapter we asked how it could possibly happen that the world would rise to embrace the appearance of the antichrist, the little horn of Daniel. Now we know. It is through unfamiliarity on our part of the overall biblical pattern hidden in the Bible. Most will think that the Gog/Magog war is the Battle of Armageddon and will mistake the timing of the appearance of Jesus Christ. There is another contributing factor we need to discuss that helps the antichrist to deceive the world. It is the rise of the false prophet to herald the arrival of the false Messiah.

The False Prophet

There is a phenomenon happening right now in the nation of Israel that will help to perpetrate the illusion of the false Messiah and his coming to the Jewish people. Many influential Rabbis and respected scholars of the Jewish faith are saying that the arrival of the Messiah is imminent and to expect the arrival of the Messiah any day now. Many of these respected leaders have said that the Messiah has appeared to them and told them that he is coming soon.

For example, the Rabbi Chaim Kanievsky, one of the most influential leaders in mainstream Ultra-Orthodox Judaism, has said that the coming of the Messiah is imminent.[41] He began his message in 2015 and continues with it today. He is encouraging Jews to make it home to Israel as soon as possible and has told his students not to leave Israel because the Messiah will be coming soon.

---

41 Adam Eliyahu Berkowitz, "Leading Israeli Rabbi Says The Arrival Of The Messiah Is Imminent," Breaking Israel News, 3 July 2015, http://www.breakingisraelnews.com/44534/leading-israeli-rabbi-messiah-imminent-jewish-world/.

Another important leader, Rabbi Yosef Berger, one of the rabbis in charge of King David's Tomb, has completed a Torah scroll that is to be presented to the Messiah when he makes his appearance. He completed this scroll as rapidly as he could because he said there is not much time left before the Messiah makes himself known.[42] After this special Torah scroll was finished it was moved to King David's Tomb. Many other influential Rabbis have been hinting at the return of the Messiah in the near future also.

While all of these rabbis are honest men and sincere in their convictions, this is not the way the Messiah is going to make himself known. Jesus said in His own words when He was alive on the earth that He would be rejected by the Jewish people, and yet another would come in his own name and would be accepted by the rabbis and other religious leaders in Israel. We find that quotation in the Gospel of John:

> I have come in my Father's name, and you do not accept me, but if someone else comes in his own name, you will accept him. (John 5:43 NIV)

Those words are literally being fulfilled in Israel right now. When Jesus Christ comes again the second time, the whole world will know about it. You will not have to be an important rabbi or a special group of elite people with special privileges. If you are alive at that time, you will see Jesus Christ coming from heaven in the following manner:

---

[42] Adam Eliyahu Berkowitz, "Special Torah Scroll Written For Messiah Completed," Breaking Israel News, 22 March 2016, http://www.breakingisraelnews.com/64082/special-torah-scroll-written-messiah-completed-photos-jewish-world/.

The False Time of Peace

> I saw heaven standing open and there before me was a white horse, whose rider is called Faithful and True. With justice he judges and makes war. His eyes are like blazing fire, and on his head are many crowns. He has a name written on him that no one knows but he himself. He is dressed in a robe dipped in blood, and his name is the Word of God. The armies of heaven were following him, riding on white horses and dressed in fine linen, white and clean. Out of his mouth comes a sharp sword with which to strike down the nations. He will rule them with an iron scepter. He treads the winepress of the fury of the wrath of God Almighty. On his robe and on his thigh he has this name written: King of Kings, and Lord of Lords. (Revelation 19:11-16 NIV)

Jesus warned us that men would come saying that they are Christ or the promised Messiah, and we should not believe them. He told us this specifically in many places in the New Testament. In the Gospel of Matthew He warned:

> At that time if anyone says to you, "Look, here is the Christ!" or "There he is!" do not believe it. For false Christs and false prophets will appear and perform great signs and miracles to deceive even the elect—if that were possible. See I have told you ahead of time. So if anyone tells you, "There he is, out in the wilderness," do not go out; or "Here he is, in the inner rooms," do not believe it. For as lightning that comes from the east is visible even in the west, so will be the coming of the Son of Man. (Matthew 24:23-27 NIV)

The person revealing himself to the rabbis in Israel is the false Messiah. This false Messiah is a shill for the antichrist. He is not Jesus Christ, but an impostor masquerading as the Messiah. Gog has released a spirit of deception in the world, and the false Messiah is another fulfillment of the spirit of deception.

The purpose of the false Messiah is to be a pawn for the antichrist, and to tell all people that they must follow the antichrist to be saved. It will be the greatest lie ever told. Following the false Messiah will lead to your destruction. Stay as far away from him as you can and do not listen to anything he has to say—even if he performs miracles and signs to verify his word.

The antichrist arises from the devastation of war and promises peace to the entire world. Many will be deceived because they are unfamiliar with the biblical patterns. Those with wisdom will see the antichrist for who he is and will strive to inform others so they will not be deceived and follow him. The antichrist promises one thing—but what he actually does is something far different. It is time to examine the storyline and pattern for the rise of the antichrist.

CHAPTER SEVENTEEN

The Biblical Pattern and Storyline for the Antichrist

The Prophet Daniel provides the background for the one who will become known as the antichrist. Instead of a pattern based on the rise of empires, the empires are secondary to the rise of a man who will control the final beast empire after Gog is dead. It seems that Satan always has a counterfeit plan that mimics what the Lord is doing. Just as our Father in Heaven had a plan where His Son died for us, was gone, but then promised to return a second time; the devil has a plan for his own chosen one to do the exact same thing. Satan will present a promised one, have him disappear for an extended period of time and then reappear on the world scene. The promised one who is the seed of Satan is paradoxically one of the most anticipated people that will ever walk the face of the planet. The Shiite branch of Islam has been waiting for him for over a thousand years.

In his description of the antichrist, Daniel begins by describing kingdoms. Almost all of the kingdoms he describes are Islamic countries today.

Daniel's fourth beast kingdom he describes has morphed into a super Islamic state in the end times, and it is from this super coalition of Muslim nations that the antichrist will arise. This super Islamic power is the renewed Ottoman Empire. There is a problem, however with the antichrist arising from the renewed Ottoman Empire. The Ottomans were a Sunni branch of Islam controlled by the Caliphate who were also Sunni Muslims. The Sunni Muslim Caliphate had put to death all previous eleven direct descendants of Muhammad embodied in the eleven Imams. They were all killed on direct orders of the Sunni Muslim Caliphate—a fact that must be dealt with before the Twelfth Imam, the antichrist, can arise to take control of the super Islamic state.

The Defeat of Three Leaders

Daniel provides us with critical clues on how this is accomplished when he tells us that the little horn, his name for the antichrist, puts down three leaders or kings from the new Ottoman Empire coalition. "While I was thinking about the horns, there before me was another horn, a little one, which came up among them; and three of the first horns were uprooted before it. This horn had eyes like the eyes of a human being and a mouth that spoke boastfully." (Daniel 7:8 NIV) The important question is: why does the little horn need to overthrow the three leaders?

The three leaders need to be overthrown or uprooted because the stronger Sunni branch of the Muslim religion will never allow a Shiite Imam to speak for all of Islam. The Shiites have always been considered a radical minority branch of the Muslim religion. For a Shiite Imam to wrest control of the

Caliphate and the Ottoman Empire must mean that a terrible catastrophe has happened and the voice of the stronger Sunni leader must have been silenced. This is precisely what will happen when the Twelfth Imam takes over—Gog and the leadership of the Sunni Caliphate will be struck down and will lay dead in Israel when the Lord intervenes in the Gog/Magog War.

Iran, a nation that is primarily Shiite Muslims, has been working behind the scenes to bring about the defeat of the Sunni majority for years. Iran's role has been crucial in bringing down the Islamic Caliphate of Abu Bakr al-Baghdadi and ISIS—the current Iraq and Syrian Hashemite leadership. The fall of ISIS will be the first of the three kings that the forces of the antichrist (Iran and its army) will bring down. As this is being written, the final push to eradicate the world of ISIS is taking place.

The next king to fall with the aid of the stealth intervention of Iran and its Shiite forces will be Saudi Arabia. Saudi Arabia is home of the woman (Mecca) that will secretly be hated and despised because of her hypocrisy and control of the Muslim religion. Gog and the nation of Turkey under the renewed Ottoman Empire will be the ones carrying out the destruction of Mecca and Saudi Arabia. But make no mistake, Iran and the Shiites will be undermining the authority and seeking the destruction of the Sunni nation of Saudi Arabia. The controlling king of the house of Saud in Saudi Arabia will be the second king to fall in the Sunni majority of nations.

The third king in the Sunni coalition of nations to fall will be Gog and his Islamic super state coalition. Iran will be part of the army that attacks Israel in the Gog/Magog War, but they will contribute the minimum amount of forces necessary to be part of the alliance that Gog assembles. Iran and the Shiite Muslims will be secretly hoping for the annihilation of Gog because his destruction will set the stage for the arrival of the Twelfth Imam. When Gog is killed attacking Israel, all the conditions will be right for the reappearance of the Twelfth Imam—the man who will become the antichrist.

The previous eleven Imams have taught about certain conditions that must be met before the appearance of the Twelfth Imam can take place. Besides teaching that the Sunni Muslims will have just experienced a tremendous defeat, they have stated that the following signs must have taken place.[43] Interesting enough, there are corresponding areas in the Bible that describe the same conditions occurring as described by the Imams. Those corresponding places in the Bible will be listed also.

1. The Imams taught that there will be much conflict throughout the land until Syria is destroyed. The Bible teaches that Damascus in Syria is going to be destroyed as a city and will be a ruinous heap. (Isaiah 17:1)

2. The teachings of the Imams were that before the one who will arise (Mahdi), there will be red death and white death…as for red death that is from the sword, while white death is from plague. The Bible describes a rider on a red horse which signifies war (Revelation 6:4) and a rider on a pale horse signifying beasts

---

[43] Wikipedia, "Imamah (Shia Doctrine)," http://en.wikipedia.org/wiki/Imamah_(Shia_doctrine).

The Biblical Pattern and Storyline for the Antichrist

which can also be biological weapons like plague. (Revelation 6:8)

3. The Imams taught that the Turk will occupy the region of al-Jazira (areas in Iraq, Syria and areas south of Turkey east of the Euphrates River). The bible states that Gog will control those areas before his destruction in the Gog/Magog War. (Ezekiel 38, 39)

4. The Imams taught that a fire will appear for a long time in the east, with remnants of the fire remaining in the air for three or seven days. The Bible teaches that the Lord will send fire on Gog and Magog, and that fire will fall from the skies like rain mixed with brimstone. (Ezekiel 39:6, 38:22)

5. The Imams taught that the Abbasids (Iraqis) would be burnt between Jalula and Khaneqin (Two cities northeast of Baghdad near the Iranian border). The Bible teaches that fire will fall on the hordes of Gog near that region. (Ezekiel 39:6)

6. The Imams taught that two signs will arise—there will be an eclipse of the sun in the middle of the month of Ramadan, and an eclipse of the moon at the end of it. The Bible teaches that the sun will become black as sackcloth of hair, and the moon will become as blood. (Revelation 6:12)

There are many similarities between these accounts. Both speak of Syria being destroyed, of war and death, of fire falling from the sky and a sign where blackness envelopes the sun and the moon. These will be the condition prevailing on the earth after the defeat of Gog and his forces. It will be the time just before the appearance of the antichrist.

This is part of the storyline for the appearance of the antichrist. Most of our background information on him comes from the writings of the Prophet Daniel. If Daniel is describing the antichrist, then there must be some sort of biblical pattern that is a prototype for the coming of the antichrist. Does a person foreshadowed in the writings of Daniel serve as a type of things to come when the antichrist makes his appearance in the world? Does this biblical pattern exist?

Amazingly enough, this pattern does exist in the Bible. And what is more astounding is the person who told us to recognize this pattern. It was Jesus Christ. The way Jesus spoke of this pattern was as if He expected us to recognize this critical pattern and become familiar enough with it that we would understand immediately the gravity and importance surrounding it when it takes place. What was this enigmatic pattern Jesus spoke of when he was living on the earth?

Jesus referred to this pattern of things to come as "the abomination of desolation."

The Abomination of Desolation Pattern

If we are going to properly understand what Jesus wanted us to recognize, then we must first look at what he said when he referenced this pattern. Let's look at Jesus's words in Matthew:

The Biblical Pattern and Storyline for the Antichrist

> So when you see standing in the holy place the "abomination that causes desolation," spoken of through the prophet Daniel—let the reader understand... (Matthew 24:15 NIV)

Let's pause here for a moment so we can properly understand what Jesus is telling us. There is a lot of background information that Jesus expects us to understand when He makes this statement. Instead of going through the exhaustive related information contained in the Bible concerning these references, we are going to cut to the chase—the relevant details Jesus wanted us to understand.

First of all, what was the "holy place" Jesus mentioned? To the Jewish people and Jesus, the holy place was always a reference to the temple. That means that in modern times the temple is going to be rebuilt and functioning again in present day Israel. People may not believe that fact, but to the devout in Israel, the rebuilding of the temple is already a foregone conclusion. They have everything needed to complete the rebuilding of the temple quickly including the perfect red heifer needed for ritual cleansing of the people. (The perfect red heifer was born in Israel in September of 2018. It is needed for the ritual cleansing of the Jewish people before the temple rituals can proceed.)[44]

Next, Jesus mentions the "abomination that causes desolation" and mentions that the prophet Daniel spoke of this, and then pointedly emphasizes that the reader needs to understand what He is talking about. Most people never stop to contemplate the deeper implications of what Jesus is trying to tell us.

---

[44] Adam Eliyahu Berkowitz, "Harbinger to Messiah:Red Heifer is Born," Breaking Israel News, September 5, 2018, https://www.breakingisraelnews.com/113476/temple-institute-certifies-red-heifer/

What Jesus is trying to tell us is that there is a biblical pattern involved here, that the pattern goes much deeper than just surface level, that the prophet Daniel spoke of the abomination of desolation pattern in his writings, that another person will cause the abomination of desolation pattern to reoccur in our times in a future manifestation, and that we need to recognize this pattern in order to save ourselves and our loved ones.

It is absolutely imperative that we recognize the abomination that causes desolation pattern. It was rare for Jesus to ever implore us to recognize a biblical pattern—but in this case Jesus is adamantly insisting that we recognize what will happen in this enigmatic time.

What is the abomination that causes desolation pattern? One of the best resources we have is our Bibles. The NIV Study Bible has one of the best explanations of the abomination that causes desolation. It states in the footnotes on Matthew 24:15 the following:

> The Abomination that causes desolation: The detestable thing causing the desolation of the holy place. The primary reference in Daniel was to 168 BC, when Antiochus Epiphanes erected a pagan altar to Zeus on the sacred altar in the temple of Jerusalem. According to some, there are still more stages in the progressive fulfillment of the predictions in Daniel and Matthew; a still future setting up of an image of the antichrist in Jerusalem.

This is the biblical pattern Jesus was trying to get us to recognize. In 168 BC, a ruler named Antiochus Epiphanes suppressed a rebellion by the Jewish people and wanted to do something so abhorrent to the Jewish people that it would violate everything that the Jews held sacred. After crushing the Jewish rebellion, Antiochus went into the Jewish temple, something a non-Jew was never supposed to do, entered the Holy of Holies, a place where only the High Priest was supposed to enter once a year, and erected an altar to Zeus, a false god, in the place that was reserved for only the Lord.

This was something that was not only highly offensive to the Jews, but also highly offensive to the Lord. It was literally an abomination that would cause desolation and had to be dealt with. In 168 BC this led to the Maccabean revolt where the Jews threw off the rule of Antiochus and eventually rededicated their temple.

If this is the pattern that the Lord wanted us to recognize, then at some point in the future the antichrist is going to do exactly the same thing. How do we know this? Jesus told us to watch for the abomination of desolation pattern to manifest again. The one repeating the pattern will be the antichrist. The Prophet Daniel told us what the future antichrist will do in the following passage:

> He will confirm a covenant with many for one seven. In the middle of the seven he will put an end to sacrifice and offering. And at the temple he will set up an abomination that causes desolation, until the end that is decreed is poured out on him. (Daniel 9:27 NIV)

The seven in this passage refers to some sort of peace treaty that is going to be made with Israel for a seven year period of time. The antichrist will reaffirm this treaty, but then will move his forces into Israel when this treaty is still in force. He will then enter the renewed Jewish temple and end the sacrifice and offering part of the temple ceremony. The antichrist will then go into the Holy of Holies room in the temple and declare that he is god and that he is the one who should be worshipped. He will place an image of himself in the holiest place in the temple. This is the new abomination that will cause desolation—someone other than God declaring that he is god.

The Apostle Paul confirmed this biblical pattern in his writings to the Thessalonians.

> Don't let anyone deceive you in any way, for that day will not come until the rebellion occurs and the man of lawlessness is revealed, the man doomed to destruction. He will oppose and will exalt himself over everything that is called God or is worshiped, so that he sets himself up in God's temple, proclaiming himself to be God. (2 Thessalonians 2:3-4 NIV)

The antichrist will desecrate the Jewish temple in the future, and will set himself up to be worshipped in God's temple. This is when the abomination of desolation pattern will happen a second time and will be fulfilled. When this happens, the Jewish people in Jerusalem were given very specific instructions—RUN. The Jewish people were told to drop everything and run for their lives. Matthew recorded these instructions to the Jews:

> So when you see standing in the holy place "the abomination that causes desolation," spoken of through the prophet Daniel—let the reader understand—then let those who are in Judea flee to the mountains. Let no one on the housetop go down to take anything out of the house. Let no one in the field go back to get their cloak.

> How dreadful it will be in those days for pregnant women and nursing mothers! Pray that your flight will not take place in winter or on the Sabbath. For then there will be great distress, unequaled from the beginning of the world until now—and never to be equaled again. (Matthew 24:15-21 NIV)

When people in Jerusalem see the antichrist entering the temple they have been instructed to get out of the city, and to get out NOW! Anyone left in the city will fall prey to the antichrist. He will destroy anyone left that will not worship him or take his mark to declare their allegiance to him. Jerusalem will become hell on earth at that point in time. The Lord has prepared a place for the fleeing people, and it is to this secure location that those who want to be protected by the Lord will escape to. (The area the Jews will escape to is Petra, in Jordan. This area was known as Bozrah to the Jews and will be the place the Lord protects the Jews during the onslaught of the antichrist. See Isaiah 26:20-21, 63:1-6, Micah 2:12)

The abomination of desolation pattern is reasserting itself once again on the earth. The antichrist will be in his full power and glory, and everyone on the earth will suffer because of him. The question now becomes—what can those living on the earth at that time expect from the rule of the antichrist? That is the next thing we will discuss.

CHAPTER EIGHTEEN

The Tyranny of the Antichrist

The Bible has much to say about the antichrist and what he does during his reign on the earth. Many will assign the best of intentions to him because they think he is Christ coming back to establish peace on the earth. To others in the Muslim religion, he is their promised one and the person who is the culmination of everything promised in the Islamic religion. There will be so much despair and destruction at the time of his arrival that people will be looking for someone to rescue and save them from their intolerable plight. The world will be reeling from the destructive events surrounding the rule of Gog and his destruction while attacking the nation of Israel. The guidance and direction of the Holy Spirit and the peace He brings will be gone from the face of the earth. (This will be discussed in a later chapter.) The world will be looking for a Savior.

The antichrist will appear promising peace and order in a time when there is none. He will have a receptive audience waiting for him. Anyone who can provide a ray of hope in this climate will be welcomed with open arms.

He will begin his reign in a world full of desperation—where deceit and demonic forces rule because of the withdrawal of the Holy Spirit. He will seem to be the hope of a world so desperately out of control. And yet his true nature will soon rise to the forefront, and he will not be able to stop himself from demonstrating his contempt for any that will not bend to the force of his will. He will not tolerate any that oppose him, and his dark nature will actively move to suppress their opinions and their voice. He will quickly set himself up to be the ruler of the world and will stop at nothing to usurp the throne that is reserved for Jesus Christ.

We have not been left uninformed about the antichrist's rise to power and the way he achieves his goals. God's word is full of references about him. We need to review some of these references so we can know what to expect from him.

References in the Bible Concerning the Antichrist

Here are some of the clues we are given in the Bible that explain the nature of the antichrist more fully:

1. **He will be the continuation of the Islamic Beast Empire resurrected by Gog.** Gog set up the Islamic mega-coalition of nations but the antichrist will be the one that controls it after the Sunni leadership of Gog and his minions are destroyed in Israel in the Gog/Magog War. The Bible tells us the antichrist comes up "out of the earth" (Revelation 13:11) and "out of the bottomless pit." (Revelation 17:8) This aligns with Islamic hadiths that teach their great leader will come up out of a bottomless well

inside the Jamkaran Mosque in Iran. Their promised one is also pictured coming up out of the earth. This is not a coincidence. The references that point to someone arising out of the earth in Revelation and the Islamic hadiths speaking of one coming out of the earth from a well in Iran are the same person—the antichrist.

2. **He will be Assyrian.** Genesis 10:9 tells us that Nimrod was "A mighty hunter before the Lord," and he was also the powerful Assyrian leader who built the great ancient city of Babylon. Unfortunately, Nimrod is also credited with leading the rebellion against God by building the Tower of Babel in the land of Shinar (Genesis 11:1). Biblical scholars have speculated that the antichrist is patterned after Nimrod, an end time Assyrian who will again lead a rebellion against God (Micah 5:5). Biblical patterns reinforce the point that an end time Assyrian will devastate Israel again in the future, just as Assyrian leaders overwhelmed Israel in the past. (See Isaiah 10:5-6, 14:25, 30:30-31). Curiously enough, both Gog and the antichrist are Assyrians. Gog comes from the land of Turkey which was once part of the Assyrian Empire, and the antichrist was born in Samarra which is near the heart of the old Assyrian Empire.

3. **He rises to power through the occult, and uses the power of the occult to achieve**

his purposes. (Daniel 8:23-25) We need to elaborate on this point somewhat. The antichrist or Twelfth Imam was hidden through a process known as "occultation." (Their term, not ours.) This is some form of secret and esoteric ritual involving the black arts which hides a person until the time of their revealing. Another ritualistic black arts ceremony is required to bring the person out of hiding for their unveiling to the world. The antichrist will emerge following just such a ritual. The conclusion we can draw from this information is that the antichrist was hidden and will arise after some sort of satanic ritualistic process. This is precisely what a scripture in Daniel tells us: "A king of fierce countenance, and understanding dark sentences, shall stand up." (Daniel 8:23) In other words, the antichrist will have extensive understanding of black magic and will come to power through the occult.

4. **The antichrist will have demonic power supporting him.** "And his power shall be mighty, but not by his own power." (Daniel 8:24) He will tap into the power of satanic sources and will be so comfortable with the satanic power at his disposal that he will encourage people to get involved with black magic, and to indulge in the satanic arts. "And through his policy also he shall cause craft to prosper in his hand." (Daniel 8:25)

One thing we can expect during the reign of the antichrist is that black magic and satanic rituals will become commonplace and routine.

5. **The antichrist heals the deadly wound of the beast empire**. (Revelation 13:3) He does this by restoring the office of the Caliphate and then combining it with the office of the Imam. Gog had continued the office of the Caliphate and the antichrist restores the office of the Imam and makes it the new Caliphate. Without the leadership of the Caliphate, the Muslims were suffering from what they considered a terrible head wound or leadership void. The antichrist heals the wound and assumes control of the office of the Caliphate when he combines it with the office of the Imam. He will be the embodiment of both offices of leadership over the Muslim world.

6. **The antichrist will deceive and destroy many by the peace he promises to the world**. "And by peace he shall destroy many." (Daniel 8:25) The world will be craving peace and order after the rampages of Gog and the devastation of his armies. When the antichrist promises peace to the world, there will be a willing suspension of disbelief when his actions accomplish the exact opposite of what he has promised. The order the antichrist promises will come through peaceful deceit and will allow him to do as he wishes without interference from others.

7. **The antichrist will set up world dominion.** "Power was given him over all kindreds, and tongues, and nations." (Revelation 13:7) The elite in many nations have sought a time when a "one world order" will control the world. The rise of the antichrist will be the fruition of this desire. The antichrist will rule the entire world—but the reign of the antichrist will be far from what was expected of a world ruler. He will devolve into a blood-thirsty despot just like so many before him. The world will get the leader of the new world order—but only Jesus Christ can bring real truth and justice to the world.

8. **To demonstrate his power and control over the world, the antichrist will cause all to receive a mark of his beast empire.** (Revelation 13:16) This point needs further clarification. One thing we need to remember is the fact that the antichrist is the Twelfth Imam. All eleven Imams before him had marks or symbols that signified their power. **These marks were worn by their followers.** It is perfectly normal for the Twelfth Imam to demand that all of his followers be identified by his mark or symbol. The Bible says that this mark will be placed in their right hand or forehead and will distinguish all those that have this mark as a follower of the antichrist. He will then use this identification mark as some sort of control for regulating everything

that you need in life to survive. People will not be able to buy things such as food and basic goods without using this mark. In this way the antichrist will have power over all people, and will probably receive some revenue stream whenever this mark is employed. Somehow the symbol he uses is associated with the number 666. The Bible describes this in the following way: "He also forced everyone, small and great, rich and poor, free and slave, to receive a mark on his right hand or on his forehead, so that no one could buy or sell unless he had the mark, which is the name of the beast or the number of his name. This calls for wisdom. If anyone has insight, let him calculate the number of the beast, for it is a man's number. His number is 666." (Revelation 13:16-18 NIV) **The Apostle John warned us that no person should ever receive the mark that the antichrist demands you take**. If you do, you will be subject to the wrath of God that will be poured out in the bowl and trumpet judgments and you will be separated from God forever. (Revelation 14:9-11)

9. **He will wage war against the saints, and will overcome them.** (Revelation 13:7) It is of paramount importance that we understand what is being said here so we can avoid the fate of the saints in this category. Where do these saints come from and why is he able to overcome them? Not all of the people in

the churches are going to be protected by the rapture. There are too many people in the churches today who do not have the Holy Spirit within them and lack the guidance that the Holy Spirit can provide. They do whatever they feel is right in their own eyes. They are unfamiliar with what is said in the Bible and consequently are open to many types of deception. Those who do not have the Holy Spirit within them live by an irrational set of rules that neither justifies nor protects them when the destructive events associated with the antichrist come to pass. Consequently they will miss the rapture and are described as being lukewarm, unwise, and those that will experience great tribulation. As we review the letters to the seven churches in Revelation (Revelation 2 and 3), many church goers are characterized in this manner, and numerous warnings are given to change their ways or face the consequences of the great tribulation. No doubt these people have some knowledge of the Bible and will realize their error after the rapture has occurred. They will finally turn to the Lord but will face a horrific time and will fall prey to the depredations of the antichrist. The saints being referenced in this passage are the ones that fall into this category. They will try to change their ways and follow Jesus as best they can in their new circumstances, but they will find it extremely difficult and many will be overcome by the antichrist's wanton destruction of Christians and Jews. This topic is so important that a chapter will be dedicated to it and the "rapture pattern" will be discussed at that time.

10. **The antichrist will not regard the god of his fathers, nor the desire of women.** (Daniel 11:37) This is another point that needs further clarification. Many have said that the fact that the antichrist does not regard the desire of women means that he is homosexual. When we closely examine this passage, a more accurate interpretation may be that women have such insignificant standing in the hierarchy of the antichrist's religion that he doesn't care what women want or desire. The Islamic culture is centered around men, with the desires of women being a secondary concern. In this way, the antichrist does not regard the desire of women or give much thought to what women want. The fact that the antichrist does not regard the "god of his fathers" should be profoundly disturbing to those in the Muslim religion. This means that he antichrist is not driven by the teachings of Islam as much as he is driven to use all means at his disposal to accomplish his goals. The Bible says he will "honor the god of forces" (Daniel 11:38) and that he shall acknowledge a "strange god." (Daniel 11:39) What is meant by a "strange god?" If we combine what these two passages say, then we can conclude that some

sort of strange god is going to appear and that this strange god is somehow in control of forces that we are unfamiliar with.

11. **The antichrist will honor a strange god and a god of forces.** (Daniel 11:38-39) What are these passages in Daniel referring to? By definition, a strange god is a god that the world is unfamiliar with at this time. This god is also said to be a god of forces, most likely forces which we are unfamiliar with. Is this a reference to some sort of "alien deception" or UFO disclosure? Is the antichrist going to rise to power on the heels of some sort of alien disclosure that will shock the world into believing in some alien foreign god? We already know the antichrist rises to take power through some sort of ritual of the occult. This ritual will employ dark forces and will use deception as a means to accomplish its purpose. The minions of Satan could be posing as an alien presence to orchestrate a grand delusion that casts doubt on the religious history of the world. The antichrist, being the opportunist that he is, will use the deceptive masquerade of an alien presence to cement and consolidate his rise to power. In this way he will fulfill the passage where it says he will not regard the god of his fathers (Daniel 11:37) but will acknowledge a strange god that is a god of forces and most likely is a deceptive presence masquerading as an alien. The most recent

book that has proposed this theory is *Exo-Vaticana* by Chris Putnam and Thomas Horn. Another book proposing the same theory is *Alien Encounters* by Chuck Missler and Mark Eastman. Both books provide excellent documentation to support this theory of alien deception by demonic forces and we would encourage you to read them if you would like more information on this subject.

12. **The antichrist will be a great deceiver.** (2 Thessalonians 2:11) He comes into the world in a time when the Holy Spirit has been withdrawn and the restraint against evil forces has been removed. Deceit will rule the day and the truth will be hard to find. The antichrist will emerge promising peace, but he will promote the most war-like conditions ever found on the face of the earth. Everyone that does not agree with him will be marked for extermination.

13. **He will show signs and lying wonders.** (2 Thessalonians 2:9) The antichrist will accomplish this by the assistance of demonic forces or by the help of a deceptive alien presence which are really satanic powers manifesting a great delusion.

14. **He will cause fire to come down from heaven.** (Revelation 13:13) One of the things the Lord will do to protect the nation of Israel when the armies of Gog are arrayed against them is to cause fire to fall from heaven to destroy the coalition of Gog/Magog. The rain of fire

from heaven is a method that the Lord uses to protect His people. The antichrist will be claiming that he is god, so it is natural that he will try to mimic the power of God by doing something God has done. He will be able to cause fire to come down from the skies by the power of the satanic forces at his disposal. Satan is always trying to mimic things the Lord has done and because the antichrist is an agent of Satan, he will have the ability to make fire come down from the skies also.

15. **The antichrist will have the ability to give life to inanimate objects.** (Revelation 13:15) What in the world does this mean? How is it possible to give life to inanimate objects? Before we comment on this, let's review what the passage in the Bible has to say. "And he had power to give life unto the image of the beast, that the image of the beast should both speak, and cause that as many as would not worship the image of the beast should be killed." (Revelation 13:15) This passage most likely refers to the application of artificial intelligence which can be the result of design in high-tech labs or as the result of demonic possession. People are going to be making images (idols) and these images are going to have artificial intelligence capabilities placed within them that are demonic in nature. This is clear because when the images speak, they are going to say that people should be killed

if they are not worshipping the demonically imbued idols that represent the antichrist. This is the way the antichrist will be able to exert control over the world and his idols will enable him to discover all those that are not worshipping him.

These are some of the things that the antichrist will do when he reigns on the earth. How does he finally meet his end? That depends on the nation of Israel and the words that they must speak so the Lord will come and intervene on their behalf. That is the topic of the next chapter.

CHAPTER NINETEEN

The End of the Antichrist

It seems strange that Jewish people must say certain words to put an end to the antichrist. But that is exactly what must happen. The nation of Israel and the Jewish people must acknowledge the error of not accepting Jesus Christ when he came to the earth the first time. Until that time the antichrist will hold sway over the earth. The Jewish people will be protected by the Lord in the special place he has prepared for them, but they will never be rid of the antichrist until they acknowledge their error and say the words that will rid the world of the antichrist. What are those words?

Jesus Christ told them exactly what they must say before He will come and deliver them when He was alive on the earth. As He was being rejected by the Jewish people, shortly before His crucifixion, Jesus looked upon Jerusalem and said:

> Look, your house is left to you desolate. I tell you, you will not see me again until you say, "Blessed is he who comes in the name of the Lord." (Luke 13:35 NIV)

It was almost as if Jesus was seeing through the ages, seeing the destruction of their nation by the Romans, seeing the holocaust and all the deprivations the Jewish people would suffer, seeing their rejection at the hands of their fellowman, seeing the rampage of the antichrist and the renewed efforts to destroy the Jews, and seeing the desperate condition the Jews would find themselves in as the antichrist tries to annihilate them. Jesus was rejected by His own, but at some point in the future Jesus also knew that His people would acknowledge their error and say the words that would bring Him back as their defender and the protector of their nation.

Why are they required to say those particular words? The words "Blessed is he who comes in the name of the Lord" come from the Psalms. They are found in Psalm 118. This Psalm is a Messianic Psalm—a Psalm written about the promised Savior. These are the words that a people would say as they were acknowledging their Lord coming as their promised Messiah. These are the words that would acknowledge that the person being spoken of was the long awaited Savior of the Jewish people. These are the words that would affirm that the person being spoken of in this Psalm would be the deliverer of His people and would assume His rightful role as King of the Jews.

You can see that in the words of this Psalm. Here are some of the phrases used:

> The Lord is with me, I will not be afraid...All the nations surrounded me, but in the name of the Lord I cut them down...The Lord is my strength and my defense, he has become my salvation...The Lord has chastened

> me severely, but he has not given me over to death…The stone the builders rejected has become the cornerstone… Lord save us! Lord grant us success! (Psalm 118:6, 10, 14, 18, 22, 25 NIV)

Then the words Jesus said they must say to Him in order for Him to save them come. "Blessed is he who comes in the name of the Lord." (Psalm 118:26 NIV) When the Jews speak these words they are finally acknowledging that Jesus is the Messiah, that He is their defense in times of trouble, that He is their salvation as a nation, and that He is the only hope they have to survive the onslaught of the antichrist. When they speak those words collectively as a nation, it will unlock the final defense of Israel. The antichrist and the vast army he has assembled to destroy the nation of Israel will no longer stand a chance. The "Lion of the Tribe of Judah" will be unleashed.

The Battle of Armageddon

God's Word tells us exactly how the antichrist will meet his fate. In his final act of defiance, the antichrist will gather all the world's armed forces and lead an attack against the nation of Israel. When the Lord responds, the antichrist will not know what hit him. As he and the armies of the world prepare to attack Israel, they will be overwhelmed by Jesus Christ leading the armies of the Lord. Armageddon will not be much of a war because the armies of the antichrist will be destroyed almost immediately by the forces the Lord brings with Him. The passages in Revelation describe the Lord descending in this way:

> I saw heaven standing open and there before me was a white horse, whose rider is called Faithful and True.

> With justice he judges and wages war. His eyes are like blazing fire, and on his head are many crowns. He has a name written on him that no one knows but he himself. He is dressed in a robe dipped in blood, and his name is the Word of God. The armies of heaven were following him, riding on white horses and dressed in fine linen, white and clean. Coming out of his mouth is a sharp sword with which to strike down the nations. He will rule them with an iron scepter. He treads the winepress of the fury of the wrath of God Almighty. On his robe and on his thigh he has this name written: KING OF KINGS AND LORD OF LORDS. (Revelation 19:11-16 NIV)

The Lord and His armies descend from heaven to destroy the combined forces of the antichrist assembled at Armageddon. The Apostle John described this scene in the following manner:

> Then I saw the beast and the kings of the earth and their armies gathered together to wage war against the rider on the horse and his army. But the beast was captured, and with it the false prophet who had performed the signs on its behalf. With these signs he had deluded those who had received the mark of the beast and worshipped its image. The two of them were thrown alive into the fiery lake of burning sulfur. The rest were killed with the sword coming out of the mouth of the rider on the horse. (Revelation 19:19-21 NIV)

The antichrist has finally met his doom. The biblical patterns we have been discussing have pointed us repeatedly to this conclusion. The armies of the antichrist will be destroyed at

Armageddon. The antichrist will be thrown alive into the lake of burning sulfur and with him the false prophet. No longer will the antichrist mislead the world. No longer will he kill those that oppose him and no longer will he wage war against the Jews, the saints, and the rest of the world that survive his reign. Jesus Christ will then assume His rightful role as King of Kings and Lord of Lords on the earth. Hallelujah! Let Lord God Almighty Reign!

CHAPTER TWENTY

The Rapture Pattern

Is this the end of the biblical patterns found in the Bible? No it is not. There are many biblical patterns in the Bible but there is another biblical pattern that is absolutely critical for us to understand. It is the rapture pattern and this is probably one of the most misunderstood patterns we can discuss. Many think they know what the rapture is and what will happen during the rapture. Others think that there is no rapture. Very few actually know of the rapture pattern—and the direct application this pattern will have in our lives. If we do not know the rapture pattern, and the impact this pattern can have in our lives—then we are ill-prepared to meet the challenges of the end times.

First we must understand how the common perception of the rapture is in error. Most of us believe that if we are Christians, and are alive at the time the rapture takes place, that we will be taken by the Lord to be with Him before things get really bad on the earth during the time of tribulation. That is a viewpoint that is commonly taught in churches that believe in the rapture and the viewpoint espoused in many popular books concerning the rapture.

The problem is that this is not what the Lord has laid out in the rapture pattern. It may be comforting, it may be the popular view, but it is not what the Lord has depicted in the rapture pattern. Most of us think that if you are a Christian, truly a Christian, and you do many fine works and prophesy in His name, and cast out devils and are a devoted church goer—then that is all that is needed to be taken by the Lord in the rapture.

Jesus's words would indicate otherwise. In fact he told us this unequivocally in His Word:

> Not everyone who says to me "Lord, Lord," will enter the kingdom of heaven, but only the one who does the will of my Father who is in heaven. Many will say to me on that day, "Lord, Lord, did we not prophesy in your name and in your name drive out demons and in your name perform many miracles?" Then I will tell them plainly, "I never knew you. Away from me you evildoers!" (Matthew 7:21-23 NIV)

To most of us, Jesus's words in this passage are somewhat shocking. Isn't this what we are supposed to be doing? Is this an anomaly? Does Jesus really mean what He says here? Perhaps this refers only to the people that were living during the time when Jesus walked the earth? Maybe we are not doing as well in this day and age as we thought we were. Is there any place in God's Word where we can get a report card on how we are doing in modern times?

There is just such a place. The Apostle John was given a vision of the churches in Revelation. However, when we read the letters to the seven churches, there is only one church that doesn't receive any condemnation from the Lord. The Church of Philadelphia received no condemnation. Five of the other churches were told that they were doing some things wrong and were counseled to change their ways, and one church was told to hold fast during times of severe persecution. Here is a brief synopsis of the feedback the churches were given:

1. **The Church in Ephesus** was told: "Yet I hold this against you: You have forsaken the love you had at first." (Revelation 2:4 NIV) The first love of any church should always be Jesus Christ. It would appear from Christ's counsel that the Church in Ephesus was focusing on something other than Jesus Christ and because of this they had lost their way.

2. **The Church in Smyrna** received these reassurances: "I know your afflictions and your poverty…Do not be afraid of what you are about to suffer…Be faithful, even to the point of death, and I will give you life as your victor's crown." (Revelation 2:8-10 NIV) This church can best be characterized as the persecuted church. They received no condemnation because they spent all of their time and resources on trying to survive and stay alive.

3. **The Church in Pergamum** was admonished in the following way: "Nevertheless, I have a few things against you. There are some among you who hold to the teaching of Balaam, who taught Balak to entice the Israelites to sin so that they ate food sacrificed to idols and

committed sexual immorality. Likewise, you also have those who hold to the teaching of the Nicolaitans. Repent therefore! Otherwise, I will soon come to you and will fight against them with the sword of my mouth." (Revelation 2:14-16 NIV) What was the teaching of Balaam? Balaam counseled the Midianite women to lead the Israelites astray by engaging in eating food sacrificed to idols, committing sexual immorality, and putting worldly desires over what the Lord would have them do. The Nicolaitans were a heretical sect that taught that the Israelites could do whatever they desired, and had sufficient leeway to practice idolatry and could engage in sexual immorality without consequence. The Lord said he would fight against those participating in these practices. This church was absolutely inundated with false doctrine.

4. **The Church is Thyatira** was told the following: "Nevertheless, I have this against you: You tolerate that woman Jezebel, who calls herself a prophet. By her teaching she misleads my servants into sexual immorality and the eating of foods sacrificed to idols. I have given her time to repent of her immorality, but she is unwilling. So I will cast her on a bed of suffering, and I will make those who commit adultery with her suffer intensely, unless they repent of her ways. I will strike her children dead. Then all the

The Rapture Pattern

churches will know that I am he who searches hearts and minds, and I will repay each of you according to your deeds." (Revelation 2:20-23 NIV) Jezebel is a prototype of a woman who leads a nation astray. The Jezebel prototype is found in the United States and I would highly encourage you to read the book *The Paradigm* by Jonathan Cahn. He explains the Jezebel prototype in detail with people in our country today (USA) that fit the Jezebel pattern with an exactness that is astonishing! Jezebel also taught the Israelites to sacrifice their new born children on an altar to Baal. Jonathan Cahn stated in his book that "Jezebel's strongest supporters would be worshippers of Baal, those who practiced or were in favor of child sacrifice."[45] Striking the children dead mirrors the attitude of those following the Jezebel prototype. It might also prove instructive to state why eating foods sacrificed to idols was so offensive to the Lord. The Prophet Daniel while in Babylonian captivity refused to eat food that was sacrificed to idols. Author Anne Graham Lotz stated the reason Daniel refused to eat food sacrificed to idols in her book, *The Daniel Prayer*. "Daniel also knew to eat the food offered to idols was an indirect way of giving tribute to them. Because Daniel's faith was centered on the living God of Abraham, Isaac, and Jacob, to give tribute to other gods, even

---

45   Jonathan Cahn, "The Paradigm," (Frontline, Charisma House Media Group, Lake Mary, Florida, 2017) p. 104

indirectly, would be to betray and deny his own God."[46]

5. **The Church in Sardis** was told the following: "I know your deeds; you have a reputation of being alive, but you are dead. Wake up! Strengthen what remains and is about to die, for I have found your deeds unfinished in the sight of my God. Remember, therefore, what you have received and heard; hold it fast, and repent. But if you do not wake up, I will come like a thief, and you will not know at what time I will come to you." (Revelation 3:1-3 NIV) This church is totally unprepared for the end times. The reference that the Lord would come as a thief in the night characterizes a church that is largely unaware of what is happening around them. They are oblivious to what the Lord expects of them and consequently their houses will be broken up and they will be left devastated when the antichrist comes rampaging across the world. (Matthew 24:43)

6. **The Church of Philadelphia** is the one bright spot in the letters to the seven churches. It did not receive a failing report card. This church was characterized by their love for their fellow man, their patient enduring of trials and their constant efforts to carry out the Will of the Lord. They are the one church that was specifically promised that they would not have

---

[46] Anne Graham Lotz, "The Daniel Prayer," (Zondervan, Grand Rapids, Michigan, 2016) p. 90

to endure the deprivations of the Tribulation period. "I will also keep you from the hour of trial that is going to come on the whole world to test the inhabitants of the earth." (Revelation 3:10) This means that, according to God's other promises, these people will experience the rapture and will be taken home to be with the Lord. They possess the qualities and attributes necessary to be taken in rapture. We should try to emulate them.

7. **The Church in Laodicea** was remarkable because it seems to display an attitude of indifference toward the Lord. There weren't really pro-God, but they weren't anti-God either. They were luke-warm in all their attitudes toward the Lord. The Spirit said to them: "I know your deeds, that you are neither cold nor hot. I wish you were either one or the other! So, because you are luke-warm—neither hot nor cold—I am about to spit you out of my mouth. You say, 'I am rich; I have acquired wealth and do not need a thing.' But you do not realize that you are wretched, pitiful, poor, blind and naked." (Revelation 3:15-17 NIV) The major problem with this church is that they are apathetic to the point that the Holy Spirit cannot direct any of their actions.

This is a devastating analysis of our modern day churches. Some say that this represents the churches through the ages, but then we are left in an even worse position. The last church was described as being apathetic to the point where they cannot be directed in their actions by the Holy Spirit at all. In all but one account this is a failing report card. There must be a key component missing in today's churches to produce such a dismal analysis of how we are doing. What is it? What are we missing and how does this key component lead us to the rapture pattern?

The Missing Key in Today's Churches

Clearly something is missing in many of today's saints and churches. Does the Lord give us any clues as to the identity of the missing component? Yes He does—but He does it in the Lord's own way. Jesus tells us what is missing—but you have to dig deep to really understand what it is. It is almost as if He wants us to search and study for the answer so we can truly decipher the underlying pattern behind it.

Where does Jesus describe the missing component? It is given when the Lord relates the story of the Ten Virgins. Let's review the salient points of this parable so we can understand what Jesus Christ is trying to tell us.

> At that time the kingdom of heaven will like ten virgins who took their lamps and went out to meet the bridegroom. (Matthew 25:1 NIV)

Let's stop here and do an analysis of what Jesus said in this passage. Of particular note is the fact that many people do not really analyze this parable because they are not virgins, so they think this parable does not apply to them. If you do this, you are missing the point entirely. The term "virgins" in this parable is referring to those that are spiritually pure—in other words they have not worshipped any other God than Jesus

Christ. They are Christians in that sense. Jesus is their Lord, and Him only have they worshipped. The Lord has made it quite clear that worshipping any other god is one of the most glaring offenses to Him. This is referred to as spiritual fornication and there are many references in God's Word where it is condemned. (Ezekiel 6:9, Isaiah 26:13, Isaiah 42:17) These virgins, we can conclude, are spiritually pure, are professing Christians, and have only worshipped Jesus Christ.

What is meant by the term "lamps" in this parable? The lamps have a deeper meaning other than just a means to provide light. If we look at God's Word to interpret the meaning of the lamps we are given the following insight. In Psalms we are told the following: "Your word is a lamp for my feet, a light on my path." (Psalm 119:105 NIV) Therefore, the deeper meaning is that the lamps represent the Word of God. Being familiar with the Word of God (Bible) is critical for any believer. We absolutely need to know what the Lord has said in the Bible. If we do, then this parable tells us that God's Word will be a lamp in our lives and will light the way in times of darkness.

The bridegroom in this parable is Jesus Christ. That fact is made clear in Revelation 19:7-9 where it speaks of the marriage of the Lamb. The marriage supper of the Lamb is prepared for Christ's church and for His saints. In Revelation it says: "Blessed are they which are called unto the marriage supper of the Lamb." (Revelation 19:9) For the wise virgins, this is going to be an event that brings true blessings in their lives.

Let's continue on with the parable. "Five of them were foolish, and five were wise. The foolish ones took their lamps but did not take any oil with them. The wise ones, however, took oil in jars along with their lamps." (Matthew 25:2-4 NIV)

This begs the question, what constitutes being wise in the eyes of the Lord? True wisdom and being wise is defined precisely in Matthew.

> Therefore everyone who hears these words of mine and puts them into practice is like a wise man who built his house on a rock. (Matthew 7:24 NIV)

That means that being wise consists of two things: Hearing the sayings of Jesus and then doing them. How do we hear the sayings of the Lord? The way we do that is by reading and studying the Bible. This is a real problem in the church today. Countless surveys have shown that over fifty per cent of today's church members don't ever read the Bible except while in church. They don't know what God's Word says because they don't read the Bible. It is nearly impossible to influence people with biblical principles when they are totally unfamiliar with what those words of wisdom are.

Likewise, being foolish is also defined in God's Word. "But everyone who hears these words of mine and does not put them into practice is like a foolish man who built his house on sand. The rain came down, the streams rose, and the winds blew and beat against that house, and it fell with a great crash." (Matthew 7:26-27 NIV) Someone who is foolish hears the Word of God, but then they do not put anything they have heard into practice. Because of this they are going to miss out on the key component that we all need in our lives. The foolish virgins have no oil in their lamps.

What does the oil represent? The oil represents the Holy Spirit of the Lord. (Zechariah 4:6) When you don't read the Bible, you are missing out on the guidance and direction of the Holy Spirit, which is represented by the oil in the lamps. **The Holy Spirit is the key component that is missing in today's churches.** The Holy Spirit has been overlooked by an unfortunate majority of Christians because they do not live their lives in a manner that will enable them to receive the guidance and direction of the Holy Spirit. In essence, there is no oil in their lamps.

What are the main things that cause us to miss out on the guidance and direction of the Holy Spirit from what we have learned so far?

1. We don't read our Bibles. We are either too busy or too preoccupied with other matters to take the time to study and contemplate God's Word. The easiest way for the Lord to influence us is during those times when we are studying His Word. There are thousands of examples of perplexing problems facing people in the Bible and how the Lord would have us deal with these problems. When we ask questions about problems we are facing and then read the Word of God, the Holy Spirit can direct us to places in the Bible where those same problems were dealt with. In this way we can receive guidance from the Holy Spirit. If we don't read the Word of God, we are missing out on this key resource.

2. We don't take time to talk to the Lord in prayer. How can you know someone if you never talk to them? That is one of the most tragic things in the Parable of the ten virgins. At the end of the parable the Lord tells the

foolish virgins that were shut out from His presence that he never knew them. "Truly I tell you, I don't know you." (Matthew 25:12 NIV) These virgins (the foolish Christians in the church today) had never cultivated a relationship with Jesus through prayer so they are virtual strangers to the Lord. When the Lord comes to take His own with Him, it is doubtful He will take someone that has no relationship with Him.

3. We don't put the Word of God into practice. If we fail to put the things we have learned in the Bible into action, then do we really believe them? If we really believe the things in God's Word, then we as individuals should have a transforming relationship with all those around us. Richard Stearns in his book *The Hole in Our Gospel* gave us an example of what God expects of us. He said: "The gospel itself was born of God's vision of a changed people, challenging and transforming the prevailing values and practices of our world. Jesus called the resulting new world order the "kingdom of God" and said that it would become a reality through the lives and deeds of His followers."[47] We need to be the agents of change in the world today.

4. We fail to do the will of our Father in Heaven. Only the Holy Spirit can guide us and direct

---

47   Richard Stearns, "The Hole in Our Gospel," (World Vision Inc, Thomas Nelson, Nashville, Tennessee, 2009) pp. 2-3

us on the path to do what our Heavenly Father wants us to do. How do we receive directions from the Holy Spirit? Any person in any church that acknowledges Jesus Christ as their Savior can receive the free gift of the Holy Spirit. After acknowledging Jesus Christ as your Savior, you can ask for the guidance and direction of the Holy Spirit each day in prayer. The gift of the Holy Spirit comes with a price. You have to give up all of your secret sins. You have to give up all those things that are more important to you than Jesus Christ; you have to give up your head-strong ways of doing things your own way regardless of what the Spirit is telling you to do; and you have to be willing to repent and say that you are a sinner and acknowledge that Jesus Christ is the only way which will ever get you to heaven. The key is having the Holy Spirit within you to guide and direct your path.

The end of the Parable of the Ten Virgins results in the foolish virgins being shut out from the presence of the Lord. They did not have the Holy Spirit represented by the oil within them. Consequently they missed out on being with the Lord. The parable concludes with the following devastating words:

> And while they went to buy, the bridegroom came; and they that were ready went in with him to the marriage; and the door was shut. Afterward came also the other

virgins, saying, Lord, Lord, open to us. But he answered and said, Verily I say unto you, I know you not. (Matthew 25:10-12)

These are probably some of the most tragic words people calling themselves a Christian can ever hear—the Lord telling you that he never knew you. It's a devastating assessment to have the Lord say that he never knew you—and it's something that doesn't have to happen.

Having the Holy Spirit within you as a Christian is the key component missing in many of today's churches. In fact, the one giving the assessment to each of the seven churches in Revelation was the Holy Spirit. Each letter to a church contains the words "hear what the Spirit says to the churches." The Holy Spirit should be an integral part of every believer's life.

Why is so much emphasis being placed on the Holy Spirit? **It's because the Holy Spirit is the foundation and the key component of the rapture pattern.**

The Rapture Pattern

Before we clarify the rapture pattern, we need to ask an important question. Why does the rapture take place? After all, weren't the Jews the chosen people of the Lord—why weren't they saved by a rapture-like pattern? Does the Lord love Christians more than he loves the Jewish people? What's the difference?

It has to do with what is removed from the earth during the rapture. This is a point that has never been adequately explained during all the years of rapture debate. The Holy Spirit is going to be removed from the earth during the rapture. The Holy Spirit came to the world at a specific time with the birth of the church on the day of Pentecost. (Acts 2:1-4) The Holy Spirit will leave the world at a specific time also. The Apostle Paul told us that there was a secret power of lawlessness at work in the world, but the one who holds it back (Holy Spirit) would continue to hold it back until He is taken out of the way. (2 Thessalonians 2:7) Only the Holy Spirit can restrain lawlessness and the Holy Spirit is going to be removed from the earth during the rapture.

The people who are going to be removed during the rapture have a very specific characteristic about them. They have the gift of the Holy Spirit within them. The Holy Spirit dwells within them to the point that the Holy Spirit is an integral part of who that person is. The Holy Spirit is part of their essential being to the point that they are indistinguishable from the Holy Spirit in their actions. It doesn't mean they are perfect and without faults and sin, but the Holy Spirit guides and directs their actions representing Jesus Christ and He acts through them. **The Lord cannot exercise judgment on Himself, and those with the Holy Spirit within them must be removed before judgment can take place. This is the reason for the rapture.**

When the Holy Spirit leaves, He will be taking those that have the gift of the Holy Spirit inside them with Him. The rapture removes those with the Holy Spirit residing inside them from the earth, leaving the world vulnerable to the destructive events that come during the judgment that follows.

The Prototype Example

If the rapture pattern truly exists then there must be an example of it in God's Word that we can study and examine. There is an example in God's Word of a person being taken to be with the Lord. It is found in the Book of Kings. The Prophet Elijah had spent years doing the Will of the Lord and finally it was time for him to be with the Lord. Instead of dying, the Lord sent chariots of fire to physically pick Elijah up and take him to heaven. Here is an account of what happened:

> As they were walking along and talking together, suddenly a chariot of fire and horses of fire appeared and separated the two of them, and Elijah went up to heaven in a whirlwind. (2 Kings 2:11 NIV)

Why did the Lord take Elijah to heaven in this manner? It established the prototype of the rapture pattern. Elijah was taken to be with the Lord in a flaming chariot and a whirlwind. Since this is the prototype of what we can expect in the rapture pattern, then the rapture is not going to be a benign event where people simply disappear from the face of the earth. The Lord is going to send His Heavenly Messengers to collect these individuals in chariots of flaming fire with whirlwinds accompanying them. It will be hard not to notice what is happening at that time. When the collection of those who are raptured is finished, people will know that a major event has just taken place.

This mimics the pattern of when the Holy Spirit first appeared. The Holy Spirit appeared on the day of Pentecost and was described in this way:

> Suddenly a sound like the blowing of a violent wind came from heaven and filled the whole house where they were sitting. They saw what seemed to be tongues of fire that separated and came to rest on each of them. All of them were filled with the Holy Spirit... (Acts 2:2-4 NIV)

The same elements are there. The violent wind sounds and the tongues of fire. This further links the rapture pattern with the presence of the Holy Spirit.

This is the rapture pattern. It makes many of the arguments about rapture timing irrelevant. When the Holy Spirit leaves the earth, you will be going with Him if you have the Holy Spirit within you. Instead of worrying about the timing of the rapture, we should be concentrating on the fruit of the Spirit.

This concept is so important that we should be putting more emphasis on the characteristics of those that have the Holy Spirit within them. What does this look like in our every-day world? The Apostle Paul tells us how to recognize someone that has the Holy Spirit within them.

> But the fruit of the Spirit is love, joy, peace, forbearance, kindness, goodness, faithfulness, gentleness and self-control. Against such things there is no law. (Galatians 5:22-23 NIV)

Likewise, there are ways to tell if you do not have the Holy Spirit within you. Paul tells us those characteristics also:

> The acts of the flesh are obvious: sexual immorality, impurity and debauchery; idolatry and witchcraft;

hatred, discord, jealousy, fits of rage, selfish ambition, dissensions, factions, and envy; drunkenness, orgies and the like. I warn you, as I did before, that those who live like this will not inherit the kingdom of God. (Galatians 5:19-21 NIV)

The rapture pattern is set. Too many Christians today think that if they profess to be Christians, then they can do whatever they like, just as long as they have good reasons to justify their actions, and they will be taken by the Lord during the rapture. It's like a "get out of tribulation free card" that leaves them vulnerable and not exhibiting any of the characteristics that are so needed in today's world. Many people have no idea that these people are Christians because they are not examples of what Jesus Christ would have them to be. They are like salt that has lost its savor or a light placed under a bushel.

These are the saints that will be overcome when the antichrist holds dominion over the earth.

What about the United States? Where does America stand in light of the biblical patterns we have discussed? America isn't mentioned in the Bible, but are biblical patterns manifesting in the United States today? That is what we will discuss next.

CHAPTER TWENTY-ONE

America in Biblical Patterns

For those of us living in the United States, there has always been of question of where exactly we fit into end time events. Many have tried to force America into Bible prophecy, but we simply do not fit. Most of biblical stories are centered on the nation of Israel, with the exception being the journeys that the Apostle Paul took as he was spreading the message of the gospel in the Mediterranean Sea area and the Middle East. Even the seven churches written about in Revelation were all firmly located in the modern day nation of Turkey. America seems like a distant land—and a place where the events of the Bible seem far removed. Yet even with our geographical distance, the Lord has a way of reaching out to us and including us in end time events. How does He do that?

The United States is not mentioned in biblical prophecy, but that does not mean that our nation is not included in a series of biblical patterns that are relevant to us today. All nations fall under the watchful gaze of our Heavenly Father, and likewise all nations can be rebuked when they are doing things wrong. The nation of Israel serves as a template for understanding certain patterns that can occur when things went wrong in their past. The nation of Israel made many mistakes in their history, and others can benefit by seeing the mistakes that Israel made, and then learning from those mistakes. If we fail to learn from their mistakes of the past, then we are doomed to repeat those same mistakes in our own nations with devastating consequences.

The United States is currently on the path of repeating the same deadly mistakes that Israel made in their past. And much like Israel in the past, we too are blissfully unaware of the consequences of our actions. Our attitude nationally is much more like we are defiantly unaware of our mistakes—and determined to proceed forward regardless of the consequences.

When a nation develops an attitude of hostility and indifference toward God, while still outwardly professing a belief in the Lord, then they are on the same shaky ground that Israel found itself in many years ago. What are we referring to?

After the reign of King David and King Solomon, the nation of Israel began to break apart. Eventually Israel split into two separate nations with ten of the tribes going north and forming the nation of Samaria, and two of the tribes staying south. The two southern tribes formed their nation with the capitol city of Jerusalem and the tribe of Judah (Jews) dominating their government.

We are going to focus on the ten tribes forming the nation of Samaria because they are an appropriate example for us to learn from and similar to the United States in many ways. The ten tribes that formed Samaria had once dedicated themselves to God, but then distanced themselves from Him and began to ignore the power that once made them great. The United States is very similar to the ten northern tribes and the nation of Samaria in that regard. Our nation was founded on Christian principles and the Lord was the center of our way of life when we were a younger nation. But much like the Samaritans, we began to move slowly away from the Lord with many of our actions. Now we are a nation that bears little resemblance to the country we once were.

It is instructive for us to recognize the patterns that began to manifest in Samaria before judgment fell on the ten northern tribes. They had once been a part of a great nation that was strong militarily. The united kingdom of Israel under King David and later King Solomon had dominated the entire region around them. The military forces of Israel had subdued all the powerful countries around them and enjoyed an unparalleled time of peace and prosperity. But then several things began to happen that weakened their entire nation. These are some of the factors that led to the downfall of the nation of Israel, and the Samaritan nation in particular.

1. An era of political divisiveness began to dominate the governmental landscape. This divisiveness became so great that the nation split in two and the ten tribes relocated their government to the north and formed the nation of Samaria. Samaria became a shadow of what they had formerly been, and the last vestiges of what had made them once great were systematically removed from their society. The detrimental effects of these actions soon began to manifest in their society.

2. The Samaritans turned away from God. Their attitude of complacency toward God soon became indifference toward Him, and then this attitude was soon replaced by spiritual confusion and then outright hostility toward the Lord. This soon became a pattern of rejection of the ways of the Lord, and these attitudes were reflected in their society by openly condemning any values given to them by the Lord and holding these values in contempt. They began to mock the Lord and began to embrace vulgar and profane values that soon permeated their society. They became brazen in their attacks against the Lord.

3. They began to outlaw the Ten Commandments and anything that would remind them of their religious roots. The Ten Commandments were never spoken of in the Samaria and the Torah was forgotten by their people in general. Their religious rituals were replaced by ceremonies to different gods that were common in the societies around them and they began to adapt the attitudes of the people that had once been their enemies and had sought to destroy them. The values that had once defined the Samaritans were discarded and soon replaced by depraved and hostile attitudes toward anything that reminded them of the Lord.

4. The Samaritans began the outright persecution of those faithful to God. It wasn't enough to merely reject the Lord, they soon began to

attack and marginalize those in their society that did not reflect their same attitude of hostility toward God. Those who spoke the name of God in the Samaritan society were open to mockery and attack. Anyone faithful to the Lord could have their property seized and their possessions confiscated. (See the example of Naboth and his vineyard that was seized by King Ahab in 1 Kings 21.) The Samaritans became a society that was intolerant toward those who were faithful to God, and yet very tolerant of those exhibiting perverse or aberrant behavior or attitudes. They became a society that was so openly hostile to God that they became like the enemies of God in their thoughts and actions.

5. The Samaritans began worshipping idols. As hard as this is to believe, the Samaritans not only rejected the Lord, but they soon replaced Him with the gods of those in the countries surrounding them. Baal worship became commonplace among them, and one of the Samaritan kings (Ahab) married a Baal worshipping queen (Jezebel). Because of this, the practices of Baal worship became deep seated in the Samaritan society, and with it one of the most egregious offenses to the Lord, the practice of child sacrifice, became widespread and openly practiced by the Samaritans.

6. The Samaritans openly embraced infanticide. The way this was carried out is almost too

gruesome to even contemplate. Samaritan women would take their new-born infants to a place where a metal idol dedicated to Baal was erected. The Baal idol would have a fire roaring inside of it and had a pair of outstretched arms reaching out in front of it that would be glowing red hot from the heat of the fire inside the idol. The mothers would then give their babies to the prophets of Baal who would place the babies on the arms of the red-hot Baal idol where they would suffer an appalling death. In this manner the Samaritan women would be declaring their allegiance to Baal. This was a transgression of the moral code that was so offensive that it could not be overlooked by God.

By their actions and attitudes, the ten tribes of Israel that comprised the Samaritan nation moved into a period of judgment by the Lord. No longer would they have His blessings and His protective hand looking over them. Their protection was removed, and the enemies that had long sought to destroy them were held back no more. The Samaritans were going to experience something they had never endured before—but even in the midst of the destructive patterns that would soon overwhelm them, the Lord held out His hand for them to return to Him.

Two destructive patterns would manifest and appear as a sign to the Samaritan people. These two patterns would reverse if the Samaritan people would return to the Lord. These two patterns would determine the fate of their nation because these two patterns would manifest to any nation that had once dedicated themselves to the Lord but had strayed from their path. **These two patterns manifested in Samaria, and these two patterns have already appeared in the United States also.** Samaria ignored these two patterns and went on to be destroyed by their enemies—the question remains; what will the United States do? Will we be destroyed by our enemies, or will we return to the Lord, repent of our sins, and seek the face of the One who wishes to bless us again as a nation?

We might also ask why these destructive patterns are manifesting in the United States. Aren't we separate from Israel and the break-away country of Samaria? Why should these same things happen to us also?

The simple fact of the matter is that the United States was formed using the pattern of Israel as the basis for our government. The principles found in the Declaration of Independence and the Constitution were borrowed from the Ten Commandments and the ideals encapsulated in Israeli society. The idea that people as individuals had rights was a God inspired idea, not something found among the governments of men. Governments have a tendency to restrict our rights, while the Lord wanted to give us more freedom and additional rights as individuals. **Because we are a nation formed after the pattern of Israel, by the patterns manifested in Israel we can suffer judgment also when we turn away from the Lord.**

So you can be as informed as possible, let's take a look at the two destructive patterns that manifested in Samaria, and have now appeared in our country also.

The Two Destructive Patterns

The person who first wrote of these destructive patterns was Jonathan Cahn. In his ground-breaking work called *The Harbinger*, Jonathan described the first destructive pattern that struck Samaria and then struck the United States also. It began with a breach of the defenses of the country. In this event, the enemies of the country perpetrated an unexpected attack on the walls of the city that left the country reeling and made them realize that they were vulnerable to an attack of far greater magnitude that could eventually destroy their nation. The initial breach of their defenses was followed by a series of warnings or harbingers that warned the nation that further destructive events lay in store for them unless they changed their ways. The nation's response to these warnings determined the fate that was in store for them.

In the next destructive pattern, the Lord provided a last-ditch effort to bring the people that had once revered Him so much back to Him. We call this the "reprieve pattern" and Jonathan Cahn called it *The Paradigm* in his book of the same name. In the reprieve pattern, the Lord chooses a man to right some of the wrongs a country is doing, and to return the country to a path where they had achieved renown in the past. This is a last ditch effort by the Lord and a final warning to a people and nation to return to Him or they will suffer the consequences of their actions. This will manifest as a destructive pattern because a series of "Chaos Events" will occur during the reprieve pattern if the people fail to heed the warnings of the Lord. These Chaos Events will serve as a preview of what will happen eventually to that country if they continue unabated on their course. **When the man chosen to lead in the reprieve pattern is removed from power, no more warnings will be**

given to that nation and they will enter a time of judgment if they have not returned to the Lord. This means a time of destruction will fall on that nation and they will cease being a nation. Then the warnings portrayed in the Chaos Events will overwhelm their entire country on a national scale with devastating consequences.

These are the two destructive patterns that appeared in Samaria before they were destroyed as a nation. How and when have these two patterns manifested in the United States?

The First Destructive Pattern in the United States

The first destructive pattern, the breach of our defenses, took place on 9/11 in 2001. We were totally unprepared for an attack of this nature. The enemies of this country used our own planes against us to strike the Twin Towers in New York. In the aftermath of the attacks, the Twin Towers collapsed and portions of the Pentagon lay in ruins. When the dust and smoke had cleared, over 2900 Americans lay dead in the ruble.

Our response to this tragedy was much like the Samaritans in ancient Israel. We were incensed and vowed to rebuild all that was lost. We defiantly rebuilt and determined to get even with those that had wronged us—even as a series of warnings or harbingers manifested much like they had in Samaria of old. We failed to heed the warnings of the harbingers and proceeded steadfastly on a course that did not return us to the Lord. The warnings became stronger and we became more belligerent in our attitude of defiance. We continued to ignore God and refused to turn to him in our time of adversity.

Using Biblical Patterns To Unlock End Time Events

There is a natural progression of events that signals when a society is proceeding to a point of judgment by the Lord. The United States exhibited all of those signs in the year 2015. We had lost our way. The political parties were at war with each other, the economy was floundering, more Americans were on food stamps than at any other time in our history and we were sprinting away from our Christian values at a record pace. Christianity was being mocked on television and in the movies. Attitudes that debased our society were being championed by many and held up as a standard for which we should be striving to achieve.

It was at this time that many different people began to notice an unusual pattern of signs that was pointing to a particular period of time on the horizon. This was when I first began to notice a system of interconnected patterns that were in the Bible. The more I studied these patterns, the more I began to notice how these patterns were re-manifesting in our time. I discovered a war-pattern that was hidden in the Bible, and discovered the signs that usually accompanied this war-pattern. What was significant to me was the fact that this war pattern could reappear at any time, but in some ways seemed to be connected to the series of signs that would appear in September of 2015.

I published my first book on the patterns I had recognized in April of 2015. The book was called *Fifteen Days in September That Will Change the World*. My intention was to lay out the evidence for the war patterns that would soon take place in the nation of Israel's future and to make people aware of the once in a lifetime pattern of signs that would be manifesting from September 13th, 2015—the date of the Shemitah judgment—to September 28th, 2015 when the final blood moon would be manifesting. I laid out a scenario of possible judgment that could occur in the United States that I hoped would never happen. I think it was the answer to many prayers that the proposed scenario never happened.

Instead of judgment, the Lord in His infinite mercy provided us with a reprieve pattern that began two months after the publication of my book, and three months before the culmination of signs that signaled the end of the breach of our defenses pattern in September of 2015. (Many other books had been published around this time also that warned of impending judgment in the United States). Instead of the devastation foretold by the signs, we were being given another chance to return to the Lord.

The Second Pattern, the Reprieve Pattern, Begins

The reprieve pattern began rather inauspiciously when a long shot candidate, an outsider to the political arena, announced his intention to seek the Presidency of the United States. On June 16th, 2015, Donald Trump announced his intention to become President of the United State from Trump Tower in New York. His announcement was not taken seriously by the vast majority of people that heard it. After all, Mr. Trump was not a political insider and had not risen through the political grooming process that all candidates were expected to navigate. He was brash and outspoken and at many times his words exhibited reckless abandon and the impulsivity of the moment. He was unlike almost any other candidate that had ever run for political office and yet he displayed a self-confidence and thickness of skin rarely seen by anyone running for the office of President. He was determined to succeed even if few believed in him and displayed tenacity and strategic insight that was unparalleled in the modern political arena.

The footsteps Donald Trump walked in were foreshadowed by another person that had been chosen by the Lord to right the wrongs being committed in ancient Samaria. His name was Jehu and just like Donald Trump he was an outsider to the political arena. Jehu had no royal lineage that would qualify him for the throne of Samaria, and did not possess any royal bloodline that would make him eligible to become the King of Samaria. Yet in the time of severe national distress in Samaria, the Lord chose Jehu to become the leader of that nation. Jehu had none of the qualifications to be the King, and yet the Lord chose him to be a leader when Samaria needed him the most. (2 Kings 9:1-3)

Ancient Samaria in that day was a cesspool of political intrigue with an evil king (Ahab) and a Baal worshipping queen (Jezebel) that championed the cause of infanticide. Jezebel was the antithesis of what the Lord wanted his people to be and broke almost every moral code given to the nation of Israel. Jehu was determined to overthrow the influence that Baal had over Samaria and consequently destroyed all of the idols of Baal and had the house of Baal worship destroyed. (2 Kings 10:26-28) Ahab had already died when Jehu was chosen to be king but Jezebel was still a powerful queen that exerted significant control over the kingdom of Samaria. Jehu was determined to rid the kingdom of Jezebel's control and used his influence to have Jezebel dealt with. The servants of Jezebel threw her down from a high tower (2 Kings 9:32-33) and dogs ate the body of Jezebel before she could be buried. (2 Kings 9:36-37)

Jehu rid the nation of Samaria from the influence of Baal, but still the people of Samaria did not turn back to the Lord. They continued on the path that led them away from God until they were eventually conquered during the Assyrian conquest of Samaria. Jehu was a man with many faults and character flaws but during his reign the Samaritan people had their final chance to return to the Lord. When they did not, judgment fell upon their nation and their nation was erased from the history books. Their reprieve pattern ended most tragically. It did not have to be that way.

Donald Trump is walking in the biblical pattern established by the Lord with Jehu so many years ago. He was elected President in November of 2016 and has been divisive since that election. Amidst the controversies he has generated, he has still managed to accomplish many things of note. Although we may not agree with every decision he has made, it is indisputable that he has made an impact on the world and in many ways things have become better for us as a nation. Here is a partial list of some of his accomplishments:

1. He refuted and withdrew from a nuclear agreement with Iran that placed the nation of Israel at risk. Regardless of all the hysterics from all sides, the nuclear experts agreed that this agreement would have enabled the nation of Iran to develop nuclear weapons. The mullahs in Iran have consistently stated that they would use nuclear weapons if they had them against the nation of Israel.
2. He has recognized Jerusalem as the proper capitol of the Jewish people by moving the

United States Embassy to Jerusalem. This generated tremendous controversy amongst the nations because President Trump's action officially acknowledged the nation of Israel and stated that they have a right to exist and that their capitol city is and will forever be the city of Jerusalem. The Lord declared this long ago and it is not up to the nations of the world to dictate to God what He will do with the city of Jerusalem.

3. President Trump has calmed a nuclear tyrant. President Kim Jong-un of North Korea was lobbing missiles over Japan and across the Pacific Ocean before being warned by President Trump to stop his actions or there would be consequences. This decree forced a nuclear bully to reconsider his actions and brought him to the table where we are now having talks and making decisions about nuclear disarmament for the Korean Peninsula. Without President Trump's intervention we could be embroiled in another war in Korea.

4. He has placed language in the 2018-2022 strategic plan of the Department of Health and Human Services that defines human life as beginning at conception which lays the groundwork for acknowledging that abortion

is murder.[48] This action by the president officially sets up the framework by which the Roe vs Wade decision in 1973 legalizing abortion could be overturned by the Supreme Court. Millions of babies could be protected by this action.

5. President Trump has appointed two Supreme Court justices, 29 circuit court judges, and 53 district judges in his short time in office.[49] This is more than any other president in history at this time in his Presidency and has set the stage for crucial showdowns on abortion legislation, affirmative action, environmental issues and financial regulations.

6. He has passed Tax breaks for individuals and corporations that have revived a stagnant economy. Unemployment levels are at record lows with all ethnic groups benefiting from the increased employment opportunities.

7. The last strongholds of ISIS in Syria were defeated in March of 2019 with leadership coming from President Trump's alliance coalition. The exploits of ISIS that terrorized the world for many years has finally been defeated. The Islamic Caliphate resurrected by Abu Bakr Al-Baghdadi has been destroyed

---

48 Mythili Sampathkumar, "Trump administration officially defines life as beginning at conception." The Independent, 10 October 2017, https//www.independent.co.uk/news/trump-life-begins-conception-definition-health-abortion-is-latest-a7993576.html, retrieved 11/17/18

49 Adam Cancryn, "Even if Democrats win, Trump has them beat on the courts," Politico, November 5, 2018," https://politico.com/story/2018/11/05/trump-courts-elections-judges-960754, retrieved 11/17/18

and Al-Baghdadi has gone into hiding. The scourge that had killed thousands of people and preyed on the weak is no more.

8. President Trump has declared that the strategic Golan Heights captured from Syria in the Six Day War in 1967 belongs to the nation of Israel.[50] What President Trump did with this declaration was to recognize that the Golan Heights, currently in the nation of Syria, actually belongs to the nation of Israel. When God set aside land for the nation of Israel it was supposed to stretch from the river in Egypt to the Euphrates River. "Unto thy seed have I given this land, from the river of Egypt, unto the great river, the river Euphrates." (Genesis 15:18) President Trump is the only US President to actually acknowledge that the Golan Heights was intended for the nation of Israel in his tweet. This is in line with what the Lord has decreed which again places President Trump in direct opposition to many political leaders.

9. President Trump has done so much for Israel that some think he will be the catalyst to bring about the rebuilding of the new Jewish Temple, the Third Temple, on the Temple Mount in Jerusalem. There are biblical patterns that suggest he will become like the ancient leader Cyrus that was instrumental in helping

---

50   Jeremy Diamond and Jennifer Hansler, "Trump says it's time for US to recognize Israel's Sovereignty over the Golan Heights, CNN, March 22, 2019, https://www.cnn.com/2019/03/21/politics/trump-golan-heights-tweet/index.html

the Jews rebuild their temple following their Babylonian captivity. It has been rumored that President Trump is working with Saudi Arabia behind the scenes to help bring about a new peace plan for the region that will clear all the hurdles for the construction of the new temple and may bring some stability to this volatile region. Many in the Jewish community feel that this was the reason Donald Trump was elected President—to bring about the reality of a new temple in Jerusalem.

These are just a few of the accomplishments that President Trump has managed within the short span of his presidency. He has pushed forward with his agenda in spite of political opposition at home and widespread criticism from abroad. Many of his decisions have been in support of the nation of Israel and this has garnered rejection of his policies from almost all of the Muslim nations and many other world leaders.

President Trump does not fit the image of who we would expect to carry out God's Will, but he has done just that in many ways. Even while he is doing many of the things that accomplishes the Lord's purposes we may cringe—but we do not have to agree with all of his actions in order to support the president. He is a man of many faults and character flaws but is leading us faithfully during a time when a reprieve pattern has been declared for our nation. In many ways President Trump is a scapegoat for our own failures. We like to point out all the character deficiencies that he has while ignoring our own. President Trump did not lead us into the situation where our nation is in danger of judgment from the Lord—we did that by ourselves. In many ways the president is trying to save a nation that does not know it needs to be saved. The United States continues to march forward blissfully and defiantly unaware of the fate that awaits us if we continue on our current path.

What has been our response as a nation during the reprieve pattern time we have been granted by the Lord? Are we returning to Him or are we becoming more entrenched in the patterns of behavior that have estranged us from Him? The following example is probably the best gauge to determine how we are doing at the present time.

1. The state of New York passed infanticide legislation in the guise of "Reproductive Health Rights" in January of 2019 that allows the killing of a full term infant up to and including the time of birth if the mother decides she does not want the child.[51] When this legislation was signed into law by Governor Andrew Cuomo of New York, the legislature responsible for this act stood and cheered. The law legalizes infanticide by any definition of the term. It allows for a full term or newly born baby to be killed. During the passage of this legislation, a full term infant was determined to have no rights as an individual and therefore did not warrant protection by the state. **It seems we have walked down this path before when we, as a nation, declared that black people brought**

---

51   Liberty Counsel, "NY Law Is Infanticide," Canada Free Press, January 29, 2019, https://canadafreepress.com/article/ny-law-is-infanticide, retrieved 3/20/2019

to our country for the purpose of slavery, had no rights as human beings, and thus could be treated as property. The injustice and inhumanity of that decision left a stain on the soul of our country that had to be corrected for us to survive as a nation. Even while engaged in a civil war to determine if this country would survive, the Norther Forces of the Union lost every battle until we dealt with this grave injustice. **It wasn't until President Abraham Lincoln addressed the issue of slavery, declared that black people should be free, issued the Emancipation Proclamation, and Congress passed the Thirteenth Amendment abolishing slavery that the North finally began to win battles and we were preserved as a nation.** The new legislation allowing infanticide is now proceeding to other states where we must decide if we are going to allow this blatant disregard for human life to continue. If we do, and this legislation continues unabated, then just like the times of the Civil War—our nation stands in danger of breaking apart and being defeated as a country. The issue of infanticide in the prototype nation of Samaria caused them to be defeated in the biblical pattern, and we stand in danger of the same judgment if we do not address and correct this issue. **The choice we make on infanticide will define us as a country and will determine the fate of our nation.**

It is unclear how much time President Trump has left as a leader of our nation in the reprieve pattern granted to us by the Lord. He faces re-election in the 2020 elections and could serve as our president until 2024 if he is elected to the presidency again. The ominous part of that future date is the fact that the leader from Turkey that will be known as Gog has selected the 2024 time frame for the possible start of his world dominion. Part of that plan includes dealing with the United States in a manner that leaves our country either unwilling or unable to come to the defense of the world and the nation of Israel. The man who will be Gog has plans for a coalition of Islamic States to rule the world and those plans do not include interference by the United States of America.

The time that President Trump has left to protect us is limited. He will either be gone after the election of 2020 or the election of 2024. Either way, if we as a nation have not corrected the course we are currently on, then we stand in danger of judgment. We could lose the nation that so many Americans have fought so hard to preserve. The nation that has been such a bright light to the world may fail and be destroyed. If the United States is destroyed, then the last vestiges of hope in a world where many people are in desperate situations will be gone. Israel will stand alone when the world tries to destroy God's chosen people.

We stand at a crossroad in the reprieve pattern the Lord has granted us. A series of "Chaos Events" have been manifesting in our country to try to get us to wake up as a nation before it is too late. These chaos events are foreshadowing the patterns of destruction that await us if we don't correct our course as a nation. Let's look at some of those chaos events now.

CHAPTER TWENTY-TWO

Chaos Events

What are chaos events and are they manifesting in the reprieve pattern the United States is currently experiencing? Chaos events are highly unusual occurrences, something out of the ordinary, that are unusually destructive and should cause us to reflect on our situation and correct our course of action. In many ways they serve as a precursor or foreshadowing event that portrays what can happen in the future if a nation is on the wrong path and does not change its ways. Chaos events will happen if a nation continues unabated on a path and will lead to their ultimate destruction if changes are not made. They are feedback on how a nation is doing from a heavenly perspective. The Lord places consequences on certain types of behavior—especially when that behavior is injurious or fatal to other people or groups of people.

When we studied the biblical pattern of the beastly kingdoms, we saw several examples of how an empire came to an end when they killed or persecuted Israel or God's chosen people. Chaos events will highlight the accountability factor that the Lord expects of nations. They are a warning of future destructive events and if unheeded they will project a pattern for how a nation may be destroyed. They will continue to manifest and will increase in intensity, frequency and severity until a nation either changes its ways or is eventually destroyed.

Have chaos events been manifesting in the United States since President Trump was elected? Let's look at the following disasters and you can decide for yourself.

- Before President Trump had even served a year in his Presidency, three massive hurricanes battered areas of the United States. What was unusual about these three hurricanes was the ferocity of the winds as they made landfall. For the first time in our nation's history, three hurricanes struck with sustained winds of over 130 miles per hour as they came over land. And the new hurricane struck before the old one had even finished.[52] Hurricane Harvey struck Houston and the surrounding areas from August 17th through September 3rd and dumped record amounts of rainfall in that area. Hurricane Irma struck Florida from August 30th to September 16th and caused massive devastation. Hurricane Maria overwhelmed Puerto Rico from September 13th until later in September and took out the entire electrical grid on the island. This hurricane caused the longest sustained blackout of any US controlled area in the history of our nation. As of this date, there are still areas in Puerto Rico

---

52 Umar Irfan and Brian Resnick, "Megadisasters devastated America in 2017. And they're only going to get worse," Vox, March 26, 2018, https://www.vox.com/energy-and-environment/2017/12/28/16795490/natural-disasters-2017-hurricanes-wildfires-heat-climate-change-cost-deaths

Chaos Events

that have not had power restored to them. If we look closely enough we will find warnings of impending doom embedded in these chaos events. These portents will serve as a warning and a harbinger of things to come. What is the embedded warning given by this event? *Devastating rains and winds are going to strike the United States placing homes under water and destroying the power grid from which we get our electricity.*

- As the hurricanes were finishing a new tragedy struck the United States. A gunman opened fire on attendees of a fall music festival in Las Vegas on October 1st, 2017. Before he was finished, 58 people were killed and 489 people were wounded in the shooting. This was the largest mass shooting in the history of our country. What was the embedded message of this chaos event? *Americans are going to be shot and lay dead in the streets.*

- In the summer of 2018 the western states of our country were on fire. Devastating wildfires struck Washington, Oregon, Idaho, Montana and California. What made these fires so devastating were the winds that accompanied them. Fires reaching the tree tops swept through many of our national forests covering vast areas of the western United States with thick smoke layers. Countless numbers of homes were destroyed in the fires. Many of these fires did not end until snow began to fall in the forests in late fall. What was the embedded message of this disaster? *Firestorms are going to sweep across vast areas of our country destroying homes and personal property as they blaze across the land.*

- Another vicious hurricane struck the United States the following year. Hurricane Michael struck the panhandle of Florida with winds that were more ferocious and intense than the previous year's three hurricanes. On October 10th, 2018, Hurricane Michael made landfall near Mexico Beach, Florida with sustained winds of 155 miles per hour.[53] The towns of Mexico Beach and nearby Panama City were virtually blown off the face of the map with few buildings left standing. Vast areas of the state of Florida were blown away leaving untold devastation in the wake of this Hurricane. What was the embedded message of this storm? *American cities are going to be blown away with such profound destruction that few buildings will be left standing.*

- There was something unusual about Hurricane Michael. It seemed to contain an ominous portent for the United States. It formed over Central America, strengthened into a hurricane over the Gulf of Mexico, and devastated two cities in Florida with Central American names (Panama City and Mexico Beach) as it made landfall in Florida. It was almost as if this hurricane was warning us that a storm was arising in Central America from Panama to Mexico that would soon

---

53 Wikipedia, "Hurricane Michael," https://wikipedia.org/wiki/Hurricane_Michael

threaten the United States. As Hurricane Michael began forming in Central America, a migrant caravan began forming at the same time. In the city of San Pedro Sula in Honduras, thousands of people joined a caravan as it left for the United States border on October 13th, 2018. Along the way they were joined by thousands of other people from Guatemala and El Salvador.[54] Approximately 7000 people reached the US border at Tijuana on November 13th, 2018. While there are many women and children in this group and their plight is truly desperate, there are many others that are demanding the United States take them in. In fact they are militantly demanding that they be allowed access to the US. One organizer of the migrant caravan, Alfonso Guerrero Ulloa of Honduras, has demanded to let them in or give them 50,000 dollars per person to turn around and go home as reported by Newsweek.[55] This migrant caravan has been followed by other caravans from Central America and the US border has become so overrun by Asylum seekers that it has overwhelmed the capacity of border agents to deal with the situation as of 3/30/2019. Border agents are now stopping over 4,000 people a day demanding access to the United States. What is

---

54   BBC News, "Migrant caravan: What is it and why does it matter?" 26 November, 2018, https://www.bbc.com/news/world-latin-america-45951782, retrieved 3/30/2019

55   Chantal Da Silva, "Migrant Caravan: Let Us In Or Give Each Of Us $50,000 To Turn Around And Go Home," (Newsweek), 12/12/18, https://www.newsweek.com/migrant-caravan-let-us-in-or-give-each-us-50000-turn-around-and-g0-home-1255043

the embedded message of this chaos event? *The southern border of the United States is going to be overrun by people demanding access to our country.*

- In Northern California in November of 2018, a series of wildfires began to rampage across the forests. One of these fires, called the Camp Fire, became a fast moving firestorm driven by 35 mph winds. The fire became a blazing inferno with 150 foot tall walls of fire driven by the ferocious winds and 2,000 degree temperatures. This wall of flame literally engulfed the city of Paradise, California and within minutes burnt the entire city out of existence.[56] This is the first time in recent history where an entire town was burnt to the ground and hundreds of people died. What was the potential message of this chaos event? *Entire cities in the United States will be burnt out of existence killing many of the inhabitants of those cities.*

- In the spring of 2019, nearly every town along major waterways in the central United States is under water from massive floods that are inundating entire cities. Twenty one cities in Nebraska and many more cities in Iowa were under water during flooding events in March of 2019. Fields have become like lakes resulting in the deaths of untold numbers of cattle, chickens and hogs, with crops being washed away and grain bins storing grain for sale and for planting have

---

56 Stephen Lam, "Everything Destroyed as Wildfire Scorches Paradise, California," (US News & World Report), November 8, 2018, https://www.usnews.com/news/us/articles/2018-11-08/whole-town-is-burning-residents-flee-northern-california-wildfire

been submerged and ruined.[57] What has made these floods so damaging is the speed with which the floodwaters inundated those cities. There was virtually no time to save the animals and farms affected by this disaster. The Governor of Nebraska has stated "This is the most widespread disaster we have had in our state's history."[58] The flooding has become so widespread it has affected oil and gas production as many of the railroads and roads used to transport oil, gas and ethanol across the country are now submerged. The flooding shows little signs of easing with widespread flooding expected until May of 2019. What is the embedded message of this chaos event? *Flooding and devastation across the Midwest will destroy animals, crops and farms and could result in famine and hunger. Fuel distribution networks will be severely disrupted.*

There have been some disturbing messages contained within the chaos events. These events are warning us of further destruction that awaits our nation unless we change our ways. We can expect rains and flooding so severe that they will deluge our cities, people to be shot dead in the streets, firestorms to rage across our country, cities to be blown out of existence, foreign people to overwhelm our borders, entire cities to be burnt to ashes, and widespread famine and hunger to strike our nation. Eventually the United States will be destroyed as a

---

57 Jason Hanna and Marlena Bldacci, "Midwest flooding has killed livestock, ruined harvests and has farmers worried for their future," (CNN) March 27, 2019, https://www.cnn.com/2019/03/21/us/floods-nebraska-iowa-agriculture-farm-loss/index.html
58 Ibid

nation unless we turn back to the power that made us great in the first place. The reprieve pattern has not ended yet—we still have time to change our ways.

What has been the most common response when these chaos events have happened? Many say that these things have been caused by climate change. They fail to see the warnings to our nation of the chaos events. Passing new laws and levying new taxes will not deal with the problem our nation is facing. The problem endemic in our society is dismissing the Lord from our lives and then continuing to expect Him to bless us in all that we do. Not only have we dismissed him from our lives, but we are actively pursuing agendas that are contrary to everything that the Lord stands for and placing ourselves on a path that demands judgment from Him.

Our Path to Redemption

There are steps we can take to reverse the course we are currently on as a nation. There is a temporary window of time allotted to us to change our ways in the reprieve pattern. There is always hope and a way that God has placed before us to return to Him. He told us of the way we can return to Him in His Word. The Lord gave us the following instruction:

> If my people, who are called by my name, will humble themselves and pray and seek my face and turn from their wicked ways, then I will hear from heaven, and I will forgive their sin and will heal their land. (2 Chronicles 7:14 NIV)

The reprieve pattern is currently in place, but the chaos events signal that we have not changed our ways and we are proceeding on a course of destruction. It is time for those of us in the Lord's church that called ourselves Christians to humble ourselves and lead the way in our return to the Lord. We must acknowledge and turn from our sins and seek the Lord and His Will in honest prayer and action. We must become independent from the society that exudes so much corruption and apostasy from God and seek to be more dependent on the Lord. We must refuse to be defined by the culture we live in and display the fruit of the Spirit in all situations. We must be defined by the love that we have for others—even as they are mocking us and seeking our destruction. We must live for the Lord, and be an instrument in His hand for affecting the world around us.

We are living in a time when the world seems to be falling apart and God is almost a forgotten idea. When apostasy abounds all around us, we must remember not to compromise will evil and lose faith. If we give in to the evil all around us we will be consumed by the darkness. If we hold fast to what God has promised us, then we will become a powerful and inspiring ambassador in His hands and one that refuses to compromise with the evil all around.

CHAPTER TWENTY-THREE

Biblical Patterns—Messages for Our Time

Many people fail to read and study the Bible today because they feel that it is an outdated message with little application to our times. In our modern world, that could not be further from the truth. When doing the research necessary for this book, it became increasingly apparent that the Lord has placed thousands of biblical patterns in His Word—and all of these patterns have modern day applications and a message for us today. **Biblical patterns contain messages that are the modern day parables of our time.** You will never find them unless you dig deep into God's Word. A cursory reading of the Bible will never reveal these patterns to you—and you will never receive the deeper message that the Lord has for us living in this time.

Many people wonder how the Lord could get messages to us today. The Bible was finished thousands of years ago and all the prophets are long dead. The last prophet recognized by the Bible was John the Baptist (Luke 16:16) who lived in the time of Jesus. Likewise, the apostles of the Lord died a long time ago. Are we now devoid of modern day direction from the Lord other than the guidance we receive from the Holy Spirit? How can the Lord get a message to us today that is relevant to our time? Do we listen to those that call themselves prophets in our day although many of them have proven themselves untrustworthy because of their failed predictions? What message can we trust is coming from the Lord?

The answer to that question is to discover and become aware of the messages revealed to us in the biblical patterns. They serve as a template of things to come, a foreshadowing of events, and a paradigm for us to watch for and learn from. The biblical patterns were placed in the Bible by the Lord, as His Divine Instruction on the way He accomplishes His purposes and as a message for us today. Any mistakes made in deciphering those biblical patterns are the mistakes of those trying to unlock the meaning of those patterns—not the mistakes of the Lord in placing them in the Bible.

I freely acknowledge that I am no modern day prophet or a person that was imbued with special knowledge from the Lord. The knowledge gained that was necessary for the writing of this book came from a series of relentless questions asked about the biblical patterns initially discovered by others in their research on God's Word. Many of the answers about biblical patterns seemed incomplete and I did not want to rely on what others had said about these patterns to serve as a final answer. I was determined to follow the path the biblical patterns showed until I had an answer to some of the Bibles most difficult questions. That included the answers to the beastly kingdom prophecies—especially regarding the seventh and eighth beastly kingdoms. Many people had offered conclusions to the identity of those two final mysterious beastly kingdoms, but most of their conclusions were based on scholarly deductions and conclusions deduced by others—not by the biblical patterns given in the Bible. I concluded the only credible answers we could depend on would be given by the Bible itself. We must let the Bible interpret the Bible. The quandary, however, is that the Bible never told us point blank who these two mysterious last kingdoms were. I began to think that I would never receive a Bible-directed answer to this question until I received the following inspiration in answer to my many prayers about the final two beastly kingdoms. The Bible may not tell us who the seventh and eighth beastly kingdoms are—but it does show us the pattern for the destruction of the six previous beastly kingdoms. The fact that the kingdom destroying the previous beastly empire was always the one that took its place in the pattern was an unrecognized phenomenon. This was the insight and inspiration that was sorely needed to draw the proper conclusions on the two final beastly kingdoms.

The answer to these questions was both an inspiration and a problem. While the answer was now apparent, the problem was that the biblical patterns were showing things that had not yet taken place. The eighth beastly kingdom has not even formed as of this time, and yet the biblical pattern has provided us with extensive information about this kingdom. Likewise, the man who will be Gog has not yet made his appearance on the world scene, and yet the biblical patterns have indicated and pointed to a man that will become Gog. None of these conclusions were based on personal perspective—but strictly by what the biblical patterns have shown.

Furthermore, the name of the man that will become the antichrist has been identified based on what was discovered in the biblical patterns. His name is Muhammad ibn al-Hasan al-Mahdi and he will be called the Mahdi, but that does us little good. We have no idea who this man will be until the time is right and he reveals himself to the world. Again, this is something that will happen in the future.

There is a war coming in Islam where Islamic factions will fight each other for control over the Muslim world. The biblical patterns have identified the players in this epic struggle and yet this too is something that is going to happen in the future and has not taken place at this time. The outcome of this struggle will prepare the path for the onslaught of the eighth beast empire.

About 75% of the things written about in this book have not happened yet, but the biblical patterns point to many things that have not yet been revealed. The Lord wants us to study and research His Word. He wants us to try to gain a deeper understanding of Him. He wants us to ask questions of Him—as one friend engages in conversation with another. He provides answers according to His discretion, and reveals Himself slowly as we gain more understanding of Him. He will never discourage us from seeking His face or learning more about Him.

This book is not a series of predictions of what will happen, but is a carefully researched compendium of what was found in the biblical patterns. The Lord is not bound by anything that man says and He is the only One who knows the future perfectly. He resides outside the dimension of time and can bring about His Will any way that He sees fit. This book should be viewed as a guide to help us in troubled times, not as the final word for how God will bring about His Will. Still, many of the things revealed in the biblical patterns are deeply disturbing.

The thing that was most disturbing to me was to write about the country that I love—the country I was born in and have lived in all my life— in a way that portrays a dark future for us. It breaks my heart to discuss what is happening in my country in our current times—and it saddens me even more to think the nation that has been a beacon and light to the entire world, could possibly be destroyed. I hope this will never happen. I hope we change. I hope we will rise up and correct everything that has been alienating us from God and will once more be in His good graces. That is my hope for the future.

The Importance of Biblical Patterns

This is probably one of the most important books you could own. Not because of how it was written, but because the Lord has a message that He has carefully crafted for you in these biblical patterns. He wants you to have this message so you can know beforehand what to expect in the future so you can protect your families and those you love.

I became a writer so I could get this message to you. I firmly believe that others were chosen to reveal the message of these particular biblical patterns to you, but for whatever reason the task fell on me to complete. Others would have been far more competent than I and far more qualified to complete this work than I. Their words would have inspired, and they would have laid out the case for these biblical patterns far more eloquently than I have. I often asked the Lord, "Who am I that I should write on these biblical patterns?" His response was always the same and provided me with a quiet confidence. "You were called and chosen to be a scribe for the Lion of the Tribe of Judah." For me…that is sufficient.

Hope for the Future

We can always have hope for the future. Sometimes we can draw inspiration from others that have endured situations far more desperate than our own. The Prophet Daniel in the Old Testament was just such a person. He lived his life in captivity. His nation was destroyed. He was one of the Jews deported to Babylon upon the defeat of the Jewish nation. He was never free, and yet inspired all of those around him by the example he set. He prayed to the Lord three times a day and never ceased being an example of the Lord to all those around him. He remained faithful to the Lord in every instance and in every circumstance he found himself in. He was thrown in a fiery furnace for refusing to worship the golden idol set up by Nebuchadnezzar and yet the Lord preserved him amidst the flames. He was cast into a den of lions for praying to the Lord when the rulers of the Babylonian Kingdom made it illegal to pray and yet he was protected by the Lord. He deepened his trust and faith in the Lord when everything seemed to conspire against him. Because of his resounding trust in the Lord, he set an example that is a pattern of behavior that we should try to emulate in our trying times.

Daniel once prayed to the Lord and offered a prayer of national contrition for all the wrongdoings of his nation. He confessed and acknowledged what his nation had done wrong, and asked the Lord to set the people of Israel back on a course that returned them to the Lord. Here are some of the words of the Prayer of Daniel.

> Oh Lord, the great and awesome God...we have sinned and done wrong. We have been wicked and have rebelled; we have turned away from your commands

and laws...Lord, you are righteous, but this day we are covered with shame—the men of Judah and the people of Jerusalem and all Israel, both near and far, in all the countries where you have scattered us because of our unfaithfulness to you...The Lord is merciful and forgiving, even though we have rebelled against him; we have not obeyed the Lord our God or kept the laws he gave us through his servants the prophets. All Israel has transgressed your law and turned away, refusing to obey you...all this disaster has come upon us, yet we have not sought the favor of the Lord our God by turning from our sins and giving attention to your truth. The Lord did not hesitate to bring the disaster upon us, for the Lord our God is righteous in everything he does; yet we have not obeyed him...Now, our God, hear the prayers and petitions of your servant. For your sake, O Lord, look with favor on your desolate sanctuary...We do not make requests of you because we are righteous, but because of your great mercy. O Lord, listen! O Lord, forgive!...O my God, do not delay, because...your people bear your Name. (Daniel 9:1-23)

This prayer changed the course that the Jewish people were on. Many Jews were released from captivity and sent back to Jerusalem to rebuild the city and the temple. Eventually the Jewish people were resettled in their homeland, and they were the nation where Jesus Christ was born and the nation where Christ walked the earth when He carried out His mission.

Prayers, repentance and a change in actions can change the course of a nation. Sometimes it is very appropriate to offer a prayer of contrition for a nation. Sometimes a prayer of contrition for a nation is the only ray of hope on a bleak horizon. Sometimes a prayer of contrition is the last hope a nation has before those that want to destroy that nation are successful.

A Prayer for the United States

With that in mind, we offer this prayer of contrition and acknowledgment of sin for the United States of America:

> Oh Lord, our Great and Awesome God, we have sinned and done wrong. We have been wicked and have rebelled against you. You have been righteous in all of your dealings with us, but we have turned from you and dismissed your counsel and have ignored you in our lives. You have reached out to us, but we have dismissed your words as something of little value. We are covered in shame for our many sins and for rejecting your ways of dealing with our problems. Your Word sets on our shelves collecting dust as the disasters in our nation multiply. Your Holy Spirit has little impact on our lives because we have covered our ears and dulled our senses with sin and have insisted on doing things our own way. Your Holy Spirit whispers to us but we are so busy we pay no attention to the things that have the greatest importance in our lives. We have thrown you out of our schools, colleges and national government and yet blame you when things go wrong. Through our greed and unaccountability, we have run up trillions of dollars in our national debt, and then placed the burden of dealing with that debt on the backs of our children and grandchildren. We have allowed our material possessions to delude us into thinking we don't

need you anymore. We have convinced ourselves that our military might will protect us from all those who seek to destroy our nation while mocking you and denying the power that once made us a great nation. We have treated people of color and different ethnicities as second class citizens and judged a person by the size of their bank account. We have been quick to judge others while failing to acknowledge our own sins. We have shown that we are willing to abandon the nation of Israel and the Jewish people and sacrifice them on the altar of world peace when it is demanded by their enemies. We have discounted your blessings and deluded ourselves into believing that peace and prosperity is somehow owed to us. We have allowed lawlessness to overtake us when we do not agree with the laws set out to protect us as a nation. We have convinced ourselves that a law allowing the slaughter of 58 million Americans is a "right to choose," and those sacrificed have no individual rights as human beings. We are shamed as a nation when the state where the "breach of our defenses" pattern happened, is now championing the cause of infanticide and cheering this decision. We have become a nation that is defined by our choices and those choices have consistently led us away from you.

We ask you to help us turn back to you, forgive our sin, forgive our pride and arrogance and help us repent and seek forgiveness as a nation. We do not ask this because of our righteousness or because we are deserving of any blessings from you because we are not—but we ask this because of your great mercy and your willingness to forgive those that have fallen. And if we are unable to turn the course of our nation—then please take those of us with the Holy Spirit within them home to you before the great and terrible Day of the Lord strikes the world in judgment. You are righteous in all that you do, and we ask these things in the name of Jesus Christ, our Savior and our Redeemer.

In the future, a time will come when many of the biblical patterns converge and the Spirit of the Lord that has been restraining evil will be removed from the world. At that time darkness will fall upon the earth and the antichrist will have full reign over the earth—although it is for a short period of time. The last hope for all will be centered on a tiny nation in the center of the world. The nation of Israel will be all alone and many of the faithful Jews will be sequestered in the stronghold prepared for them in Petra, Jordan. All the nations of the world will be coming to fight against them, but the nations of the earth will not stand a chance when the faithful Jews stand up and say:

> Blessed is he that comes in the name of the Lord!
>
> Blessed is he that comes in the name of the Lord!
>
> Lord God, Almighty—
> Blessed is he that comes in the name of the Lord!

May the Lord use the biblical patterns hidden in His Word to help enhance our understanding of Him and may He guide and direct our paths in life back to Him!

Made in the USA
Columbia, SC
15 April 2024